RAYS OF VICTORY SERIES

∞∞∞∞∞∞∞∞∞∞ ♦ ♦ ♦ ♦ ♦ ∞∞∞∞∞∞∞∞∞∞∞

RAYS OF VICTORY SERIES

∞∞∞∞∞∞∞∞∞ ♦ ♦ ♦ ♦ ♦ ∞∞∞∞∞∞∞∞∞

𝕿his Book Belongs to:

_____

(Your Beautiful Name)

"And God's peace, which is so great we cannot understand it, will keep your hearts and minds in Christ Jesus. Brothers and sisters, think about the things that are good and worthy of praise. Think about the things that are true and honorable and right and pure and beautiful and respected. Do what you learned and received from me, what I told you, and what you saw me do. And the God who gives peace will be with you."

- Philippians 4:7-9 (NCV)

RAYS OF VICTORY SERIES

∞∞∞∞∞∞∞∞∞ ♦ ♦ ♦ ♦ ♦ ∞∞∞∞∞∞∞∞∞

150 POWER THOUGHTS FOR VICTORY OVER RACISM

∞∞∞∞∞∞∞∞∞ ♦ ♦ ♦ ♦ ♦ ∞∞∞∞∞∞∞∞∞

The Power of a Christ-rooted Mindset Over Racism

∞∞∞∞∞∞∞∞∞ ♦ ♦ ♦ ♦ ♦ ∞∞∞∞∞∞∞∞∞

Readings from "Nailing Racism to the Cross"

∞∞∞∞∞∞∞∞∞ ♦ ♦ ♦ ♦ ♦ ∞∞∞∞∞∞∞∞∞

Dr. Jacyee Aniagolu-Johnson

∞∞∞∞∞∞∞∞∞∞ ♦ ♦ ♦ ♦ ♦ ∞∞∞∞∞∞∞∞∞∞

When we as the human race rise above the artificial boundaries of country, race, color, gender and creed, then we can empathize with all forms of human suffering and challenges, and we are able to become a pillar of support for one another, and one collective voice of truth and triumph.

- Dr. Jacyee Aniagolu-Johnson

∞∞∞∞∞∞∞∞∞∞ ♦ ♦ ♦ ♦ ♦ ∞∞∞∞∞∞∞∞∞∞

Copyright Permission

Edited by Uché Aniagolu (Ebony WoodHouse Productions)
Cover design by Marble Tower Publishing, LLC
Cover image: Copyright 2012 Marble Tower Publishing, LLC

Editing Style:
Please note that the editing style presented in this book by the editor, Uché Aniagolu, is meant to emphasize reverence of God, His Son Jesus Christ and His Holy Spirit. This editing style may differ from what you are accustomed to, but we chose it for the reason noted above.

First Paperback Edition
ISBN 978-1-937230-00-5

Printed in the United States of America by Marble Tower Publishing, LLC

∞∞∞∞∞∞∞∞∞∞ ♦ ♦ ♦ ♦ ♦ ∞∞∞∞∞∞∞∞∞∞

Dedication

This book is dedicated to our heavenly Father, God Almighty—a God of justice, equity and all goodness enveloped in One—our only One and True Living God, who offered us all the gift of eternal salvation through His Son, our Lord and Savior Jesus Christ.

To my dear father, Justice Anthony Aniagolu and my mother Maria Aniagolu whom I love dearly and who first taught me about God, His profound love, mercy, faithfulness and grace, and His holy justice against any form of evil, wickedness, oppression and injustice.

To all those, regardless of race, ethnicity or nationality, who need God's rays of victory to deal with and overcome racial prejudice and discrimination—may your individual victory through God's beams of justice come speedily as you abide in God's Holy Word and Presence through Jesus Christ.

∞∞∞∞∞∞∞∞∞∞ ♦ ♦ ♦ ♦ ♦ ∞∞∞∞∞∞∞∞∞∞

*A*cknowledgement

My foremost gratitude is to God my Heavenly Father for His Gift of Salvation through my Lord and Savior Jesus Christ, and His Holy Spirit Who dwells within me. It is He, the Triune God, through Christ, Who inspires and fuels me daily with His holy fire power to overcome any and all challenges, including my experiences with racial prejudice and discrimination.

To my dear father, Justice Anthony Aniagolu and my mother Lady Maria Aniagolu whom I love dearly for being wonderful parents and for all they did for me and my siblings.

My special gratitude goes to my husband, Lamonte, who remains my earthly rock of Gibraltar, and through whom God continues to teach me His expression of true and unconditional love that has no bounds. I love you very much.

My special gratitude also goes to my sister, Maryanne, a lovely woman of God—thank you for continuing to help me to better understand how to hear the true voice of God and how to spend endless quality time in God's Holy Presence through prayer, thanksgiving and worship. I love you very much.

To my sister Uché, I thank God for the sweet fragrance of Jesus Christ in you. You are an embodiment of servanthood—selfless sacrificial giving, and it is the greatness of God in you through Christ that empowers you to humble yourself to serve others; I have no doubt that God will magnify His glory in your life through Jesus Christ. I love you very much.

To my sister Chi-Chi who's giving spirit surpasses anyone that I know—May Luke 6:38 remain like a wellspring within you and may God continue to bless you and enrich your life beyond your wildest imagination through Jesus Christ! I love you very much.

To my brother Kizito whose deep and genuine love for God helps me to stay focused on Matthew 6:33; may the power of God's Holy Word continue to promote you from faith to faith and from glory to glory, in the awesome Name of our Lord and Savior Jesus Christ. I love you very much.

To the rest of my lovely siblings, Tony, Emeka, Chuka, Lolly and Nwachu, I remain forever grateful to God for your lives, individual families and accomplishments. It is my prayer that John 3:16 will be and remain alive in your hearts. I love you very much.

Special thanks to Reverend (Prophet) Michael Galleta at the Genesis Upper Room Church, San Jose, California. Reverend Michael first prayed for the success of the Rays of Victory Series manuscript and has for many years covered my family with powerful prayers of faith. God has spoken to me through him in many profound ways—and may God continue to bless you, your wife Minister Yvonne Galleta and children, and your entire congregation.

My heartfelt thanks to Minister Sarah Allred at the Genesis Upper Room Church, whom God used her prayer ministry to touch me in a profound manner. Thank you, Sister Sarah, for allowing God to use you to help me restart my walk with God, at a time when I was just a "baby Christian" who needed guidance to better understand God's Holy Word and to grow spiritually. It was under your prophetic teaching and guidance that I, in the Name of Jesus Christ, received the baptism of the Holy Spirit. May God continue to bless you!

To David and Fortune West and the Ocean of Mercy Prayer Ministry in Cork, Ireland, I would like to thank God for your spiritual covering of the Rays of Victory project through your prayers and encouragement with the Holy Word of God. As you continue to spread the good news of the Gospel of Jesus Christ, may you be a light, the Light of Jesus Christ onto nations, and may God continue to diffuse the fragrance of Christ through you to win souls.

Finally, to the Body of Jesus Christ (believers in Him and all of God's genuine priests and ministers around the world), regardless of denomination, race, ethnicity or nationality, may God's favor and blessings always overflow in your lives as you continue to spread the good news of the Gospel of our Lord and Savior Jesus Christ, and further His powerful ministry, all of which are firm-ly rooted in true and pure Love, which is God Himself.

*Y*ou, Me and Us!

Our Individual and Collective Power to Effect Positive Change

"Change your thoughts and you change your world."
Normal Vincent Peale

♣ ♣ ♣ ♣ ♣

"Let God's Holy Word give you Christ-rooted power thoughts, spiritual power and dominance that would unshackle you forever from the stranglehold of the foul spirit of racism, in the awesome Name of our Lord and Savior Jesus Christ."

- ***Jacyee Aniagolu-Johnson, PhD***

♣ ♣ ♣ ♣ ♣

∞∞∞∞∞∞∞∞∞∞∞∞ ♦ ♦ ♦ ♦ ♦ ∞∞∞∞∞∞∞∞∞∞∞∞

$\mathcal{P}$ower $\mathcal{T}$houghts Quotes

"The world we have created is a product of our thinking; it cannot be changed without changing our thinking."

"The significant problems we face in life cannot be solved at the same level of thinking we were at when we created them."

- Albert Einstein

"Men are not prisoners of fate, but only prisoners of their own minds."

- President Franklin D. Roosevelt

"The person who sends out positive thoughts activates the world around him positively and draws back to himself positive results."

- Norman Vincent Peale

"I have concluded that wealth is a state of mind, and that anyone can acquire a wealthy state of mind by thinking rich thoughts."

- Andrew Young

"You are today where your thoughts have brought you; you will be tomorrow where your thoughts take you."

- James Allen

"You have powers you never dreamed of. You can do things you never thought you could do. There are no limitations in what you can do except the limitations of your own mind."

- Darwin P. Kingsley

"Think like a man of action, and act like a man of thought."

- Henri Bergson

∞∞∞∞∞∞∞∞∞ ◆ ◆ ◆ ◆ ∞∞∞∞∞∞∞∞∞

Contents

*W*hat is Racism?

"A situation in which one race maintains supremacy over another race through a set of attitudes, behaviors, social structures and ideologies. It involves four essential and interconnected elements:

Power: *the capacity to make and enforce decisions is disproportionately or unfairly distributed*

Resources: *unequal access to such resources as money, education, information, etc.*

Standards: *standards for appropriate behavior are ethnocentric, reflecting and privileging the norms and values of the dominant race/society*

Problem: *involves defining "reality" by naming "the problem" incorrectly, and thus misplacing it."*

-- Women's Theological Center, Boston, MA, 1994

∞∞∞∞∞∞∞∞∞∞ ♦ ♦ ♦ ♦ ♦ ∞∞∞∞∞∞∞∞∞∞

*D*efinitions of Racism

"Any distinction, exclusion, restriction, or preference based on race, color, descent, or national or ethnic origin which has the purpose or effect of nullifying or impairing the recognition, enjoyment, or exercise, on equal footing, of human rights and fundamental freedoms in the political, economic, social, cultural, or any other field of public life."

-- The ICERD (International Convention on the Elimination of All Forms of Racial Discrimination)

∞∞∞∞∞∞∞∞∞∞ ♦ ♦ ♦ ♦ ♦ ∞∞∞∞∞∞∞∞∞∞

"Racism has not disappeared... we confront forms of racism that are covert or more complex..."

-- The International Council on Human Rights Policy

∞∞∞∞∞∞∞∞∞∞ ♦ ♦ ♦ ♦ ♦ ∞∞∞∞∞∞∞∞∞∞

"Racism involves physical, psychological, spiritual, and social control, exploitation and subjection of one race by another race...This means that racial discrimination and injustice are established, perpetuated and promoted throughout every institution of society - economics, education, entertainment, family, labor, law, politics, religion, science and war..."

-- Phavia Kujichagulia

(Recognizing and Resolving Racism: A Resource and Guide for Humane Beings)

∞∞∞∞∞∞∞∞∞∞ ♦ ♦ ♦ ♦ ♦ ∞∞∞∞∞∞∞∞∞∞

"Racism - Racial prejudice and discrimination that are supported by institutional power and authority. The critical element that differentiates racism from prejudice and discrimination is the use of institutional power and authority to support prejudices and enforce discriminatory behaviors in systematic ways with far-reaching outcomes and effects..."

-- Enid Lee, Deborah Menkart and Margo Okazawa-Rey (eds.)

(Beyond Heroes and Holidays: A Practical Guide to K-12 Anti-Racist, Multicultural Education and Staff Development.)

∞∞∞∞∞∞∞∞∞∞ ♦ ♦ ♦ ♦ ♦ ∞∞∞∞∞∞∞∞∞∞

∞∞∞∞∞∞∞∞∞∞ ♦ ♦ ♦ ♦ ♦ ∞∞∞∞∞∞∞∞∞∞

*T*he Reason for this Book

For every person, every child of God to know, understand and use the awesome power of God's Holy Word and His power within him or her through Jesus Christ to slay the Goliath racism that they may encounter anywhere.

"You, dear children, are from God and have overcome them, because the one who is in you is greater than the one who is in the world."
1 John 4:4, NIV

∞∞∞∞∞∞∞∞∞∞∞∞ ♦ ♦ ♦ ♦ ♦ ∞∞∞∞∞∞∞∞∞∞∞

To receive the spirit of racism is to reject God's Holy Word.
To practice racism is to disobey God's Holy Word.
To reject the spirit of racism is to uphold God's Holy Word.

∞∞∞∞∞∞∞∞∞∞∞∞ ♦ ♦ ♦ ♦ ♦ ∞∞∞∞∞∞∞∞∞∞∞

∞∞∞∞∞∞∞∞∞∞∞ ♦ ♦ ♦ ♦ ♦ ∞∞∞∞∞∞∞∞∞∞∞

$\mathcal{P}$reface

This book, 150 Power Thoughts for Victory Over Racism, is based on God's Holy Word, the Bible. The power thoughts in this book are winning thoughts for your individual victory over racism. These simple yet power thoughts will rewire and refocus your thoughts positively so that you can assume your position in Jesus Christ and take a victorious stand against racism. Meditate on each thought-provoking power thought and the Scripture verse referenced on each page, and let God's Holy Spirit minister to you.

As you meditate on Scripture, you receive it's revelation knowledge and power through God's Holy Spirit Who will reveal to you the awesome power of Jesus Christ in you and God's supernatural dominion over the evil spirit of racism (Ephesians 1:17-23). The Holy Spirit will lead you to absolute truth of God's Holy Word—God's divine stand against the foul spirit of racism and His eternal triumph over it through Jesus Christ on your behalf.

∞∞∞∞∞∞∞∞∞∞∞ ♦ ♦ ♦ ♦ ♦ ∞∞∞∞∞∞∞∞∞∞∞

∞∞∞∞∞∞∞∞∞∞ ♦ ♦ ♦ ♦ ♦ ∞∞∞∞∞∞∞∞∞∞

How to Use this Book

When reading the power thoughts in this book, please do not rush through them. First and foremost, pray the Prayer of Salvation and the Prayer after Professing Salvation. Then, pray before you start reading the first power thought and ask God's Holy Spirit to help you understand the deeper meaning of God's Holy Word that it is based upon. Then as you begin to read and meditate on each power thought: ask the Holy Spirit to help you relate each one and the referenced Scripture to your own specific experience(s) with racism, and how you can apply them henceforth, to gain positive spiritual and mind control over the evil spirit of racism and its nasty outgrowth racism.

Before you go from one page to another, that is, from one power thought to another, remember to pause—stop and think about it—Selah!— meditate on God's Holy Scripture that is referenced. Use any bible version of your choice that helps you to dig deeper into God's Holy Word. Allow God's Holy Word to penetrate your conscious and subconscious mind as the absolute truth—His Word that has the supernatural pre-eminence and dom-

27

inance to overrule the illegal activities of the foul spirit of racism against your life. Let God's Holy Word renew and transform your mind daily (Romans 12:2), and turn you into a powerhouse of positive power thoughts, so that you can take your position in Jesus Christ to gain daily victory over the evil spirit of racism. Let God's Holy Spirit minister to you through the precious Blood of our Lord and Savior Jesus Christ; let God's power thoughts become the predominant thoughts that direct your heart, mind, thoughts, will and resolve (Philippians 4:8-9)—and let them positively control your actions, responses and reactions, and influence your personality, attitude and behavior and altitude, to the glory of His awesome Name.

∞∞∞∞∞∞∞∞∞∞ ♦ ♦ ♦ ♦ ♦ ∞∞∞∞∞∞∞∞∞∞

Scripture Meditation

"Finally, brethren, whatever things are true, whatever things are noble, whatever things are just, whatever things are pure, whatever things are lovely, whatever things are of good report, if there is any virtue and if there is anything praiseworthy— meditate on these things. The things which you learned and received and heard and saw in me, these do, and the God of peace will be with you."

- Philippians 4:8-9

∞∞∞∞∞∞∞∞∞∞ ♦ ♦ ♦ ♦ ♦ ∞∞∞∞∞∞∞∞∞∞

$\mathscr{I}$ntroduction

∞∞∞∞∞∞∞∞∞ ◆ ◆ ◆ ◆ ◆ ∞∞∞∞∞∞∞∞∞

Many of us have either read or heard about the power of positive thinking, from Christian, non-Christian and secular writers. Dr. Norman Vincent Peale was a minister and author who was one of the foremost Christian authors to write an in depth book on "The Power of Positive Thinking." In this book, Dr. Norman Vincent Peale wrote brilliantly about the power of positive thoughts for daily victorious living. While, he was and still is considered to be a forerunner of Christian writing on the power of "positive thinking" in our modern world, the power of positive thinking which originated from God, was first documented in the Holy Bible, the Holy Word of God.

God's Holy Word is the original and inexhaustible source of divinely inspired power thoughts. Through the Holy Spirit inspired revelation knowledge from God's Word, many Christian writers have conveyed and continue to teach and preach powerful bibilical messages to the Christian, non-Christian and Secular world. Blessed Mother Theresa once said that she was "...a little pencil in the hand of a writing God who is sending a love letter to the world." She was very right. Through God inspired penmanship of many Christian writers, the world continues to receive "love letters" from God. Blessed Mother Teresa and Dr. Norman Vincent Peale, and many other Christian authors before and after them, who have written beautifully about God's messages to the world, including the power of positive thinking, were and are "pencils in God's Hand."

God is our Creator, the original progenitor of positive thinking—and loaded in His Holy Word are power thoughts for daily victorious living and for daily triumph over evil. The Rays of Victory Series—Nailing Racism to the Cross was written by the inspirational power of God's Holy Spirit. He motivated and guided the creation and writing of the Series based on power thoughts in God's Holy Book, the Bible, for daily triumph over the foul spirit of racism.

The 150 Power Thoughts in this book are excerpts from the series "Nailing Racism to the Cross," winning thoughts for your individual victory over racism that are based on God's Holy Word, the Bible. The goal in compiling these power thoughts is to help direct you to God's Word which will begin the process of renewing and transforming your mind against the evil schemes, intrigues and machinations of the obnoxious spirit of racism. God's Holy Word, His Precepts, are power thoughts that instruct, encourage, empower and strengthen your heart and mind—they are positive thoughts that keep you in line with His Word.

Have you faced or are you facing the fiery darts of the foul spirit or racism? Are you spiritually equipped to deal victoriously with the evil spirit of racism and its vile product racism? Do you know how to triumph over the wicked plots and plans of racists while still walking worthy in accordance with God's Holy Word? Are you operating with a carnal or spiritual mindset? Has your carnal conscious and subconscious mind been transformed into a spiritual mind based on God's Holy Word? Are you loaded with Christ-rooted power thoughts for your daily victorious living—and your daily triumph over racism?

Please come with me on this powerful journey through Christ-rooted power thoughts, revelation knowledge of God's Holy Word which gives rise to authentic spiritual knowledge, wisdom, guidance and empowerment. Let these power thoughts guide you to God's awesome Holy Word which will renew your mind and strengthen your heart daily. Let God's Word give you a Christ-rooted mindset, spiritual power and dominance that will unshackle you forever from the stranglehold of the foul spirit of racism, in the awesome Name of our Lord and Savior Jesus Christ.

∞∞∞∞∞∞∞∞∞ ♦ ♦ ♦ ♦ ∞∞∞∞∞∞∞∞∞

$\mathcal{A}$ Prayer of Salvation

∞∞∞∞∞∞∞∞∞ ♦ ♦ ♦ ♦ ∞∞∞∞∞∞∞∞∞
♥

On this day, _____, I, _____ confess with my mouth that the Lord Jesus Christ is my personal Savior; I believe that He shed His precious Blood for me on the Cross of Calvary and that God raised Him from the dead for my eternal salvation. I repent of my sins and ask God for forgiveness through the mighty Blood of Jesus Christ.

On this day, _____ by my faith, I, _____ believe that I am now saved by the precious Blood of Jesus Christ. I believe in the Triune God: God the Father, God's Son, Jesus Christ and God the Holy Spirit. I believe that in the Name of our Lord and Savior Jesus Christ and God's powerful and holy anointing by His Holy Spirit, I will receive the baptism of God's Holy Spirit that will release from my heart the flowing rivers of Living Water, in Jesus' Name, Amen.

Thank you Father, Lord God, for on this day,

_____, in the Name of Jesus Christ, I, _____ am Born

Again

Scripture Meditation:

"For God so loved the world that He gave His Only Begotten Son, that who-ever believes in Him should not perish but have everlasting life." – John 3:16

"But what does it say? 'The word is near you, in your mouth and in your heart' (that is, the word of faith which we preach): that if you   confess with your mouth the Lord Jesus and believe in your heart that God has raised Him from the dead, you will be saved. For with the heart one believes unto right-eousness, and with the mouth confession is made unto salvation." – Romans 10:8-9

"He who believes in Me, as the Scripture has said, out of his heart will flow rivers of Living Water." – John 7:38

"That which is born of the flesh is flesh, and that which is born of The Spirit is spirit. Do not marvel that I said to you, 'You must be Born Again.'" – John 3:6-7

∞∞∞∞∞∞∞∞ ♦ ♦ ♦ ♦ ∞∞∞∞∞∞∞∞

33

*P*rayer after Profession of Salvation

∞∞∞∞∞∞∞∞∞∞∞ ♦ ♦ ♦ ♦ ∞∞∞∞∞∞∞∞∞∞∞
♥

Dear Glorious Heavenly Father, thank You that I am born again by the precious Blood of Jesus Christ. I accept my renewed spirit in Him.

Dear gracious Father, I thank You for making me aware that I have spiritual and mental shackles from my experiences with racism. Thank You for revealing to me all areas where I am shackled. Thank You for giving me total release and freedom from the intrigues of the foul spirit of racism. I reject the evil tradition of racism and all that it stands for. I forgive anyone who has hurt or offended me in any manner, including my racist offenders.

Dear precious Father, I believe that You have answered my prayers in the precious Name of Jesus Christ. In the Name of Jesus Christ and by Your enabling grace, Lord God, I know that I can and that I have gained victory over any form of racial oppression and injustice.

Thank You, awesome Father, for Your marvelous rays of victory over racism on my behalf, and for Your limitless and boundless power within me through Jesus Christ, Amen.

Scripture Meditation:

"And whatever you ask in My Name, I will do, that the Father may be Glorified in the Son. If you ask anything in My Name, I will do it." – John 14:13-14

"Pray without ceasing; in everything give thanks; for this is the Will of God in Jesus Christ for you." – 1 Thessalonians 5:17-18

"And whenever you stand praying, if you have anything against anyone, forgive him that your Father in Heaven may also forgive you your   trespasses." – Mark 11:25

"Until now you have asked nothing in My Name. Ask and you will receive, that your joy may be full." – John 16:24

"Don't copy the behavior and customs of this world, but let God transform you into a new person by changing the way you think. Then you will learn to know God's Will for you, which is good and pleasing and perfect." – Romans 12:2

∞∞∞∞∞∞∞∞∞∞ ◆ ◆ ◆ ◆ ◆ ∞∞∞∞∞∞∞∞∞∞

*P*artnership Prayer

∞∞∞∞∞∞∞∞∞ ♦ ♦ ♦ ♦ ∞∞∞∞∞∞∞∞∞
♥

I commit to spending quality time in prayer, worship and thanksgiving, and meditating on God's Holy Word, to receive His powerful and winning strategies for my daily victory over racism. This I shall do only by the grace of God, in the Name of our Lord and Savior Jesus Christ and through daily guidance by the Holy Spirit. I stand in agreement with my prayer partner(s) _____ believing that through the redeeming precious Blood of Jesus Christ, God has taken away the burden of racism, its reproach and yoke of destruction from all areas of my life. I stand in agreement with my prayer partner(s) _____ believing that the precious Blood of Jesus Christ has permanently destroyed and removed the power of the burden of the foul spirit of racism in my life, in Jesus' Name, Amen.

_____
Your Name

Prayer Partner's Name

∞∞∞∞∞∞∞∞∞∞∞ ♦ ♦ ♦ ♦ ∞∞∞∞∞∞∞∞∞∞∞

Jacyee Aniagolu Johnson

Dr. Jacyee Aniagolu-Johnson
(Author remains in agreement with you)

"Again I say to you that if two of you agree on earth concerning anything that they ask, it will be done for them by My Father in heaven." – Matthew 18:19

"It shall come to pass in that day that his burden will be taken away from your shoulder, and his yoke from your neck, and the yoke will be destroyed because of the anointing oil." – Isaiah 10:27

♥

∞∞∞∞∞∞∞∞∞∞∞ ♦ ♦ ♦ ♦ ♦ ∞∞∞∞∞∞∞∞∞∞∞

∞∞∞∞∞∞∞∞∞∞∞ ♦ ♦ ♦ ♦ ∞∞∞∞∞∞∞∞∞∞∞
♥

𝒫ower Thoughts Begin...

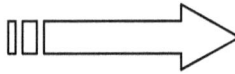

♥
∞∞∞∞∞∞∞∞∞∞∞ ♦ ♦ ♦ ♦ ♦ ∞∞∞∞∞∞∞∞∞∞∞

1

God created all races of humanity in His perfect Image, and you are

created equal, in humanity and dignity, to every human being.

God loves people of all races.

God has no favorite race.

God favors all people who obey His Word, regardless of race, ethnicity or nationality

.

God has made you in His excellent Image.

Genesis 1:26-27; Psalms 91:14-15; Galatians 3:26-29; Acts 10:34, Romans 8:35-39

2

*G*od loves you and you are special and unique to Him.

God gave Jesus Christ for you so that you may be redeemed by His precious Blood.

Jesus Christ has reconciled you to God and You are now one with Him.

If you have accepted Jesus Christ as your Lord and Savior, then you are a new creation in Him.

Through Jesus Christ you are a child of the Most High God and racism lacks the power and authority to defile you without your permission.

Jeremiah 1:5; John 3:16; 2 Corinthians 5:17-18; Romans 5:1-11, 10:9-10

3

God forgives your sins because Jesus Christ has redeemed your sins, so

nothing has the power to condemn you.

Racism cannot condemn you.

God despises racism.

God hates racism.

God rejects the tradition of racism.

You are a co-victor with Jesus Christ over every form of evil, including racism.

Romans 8:1; 1 Corinthians 15:57; Romans 5:1-11; Ephesians 1:19-23

4

*S*ubmit to God's Holy Word, reject the odious spirit of racism and its

vile outgrowth racism, and it will flee from you.

When you reject prejudice or racism, you also reject the despicable spirit of racism that originates from the devil, the father of all lies.

Racism is not God's design, purpose or will for your life.

Racism is also not God's design, purpose or will for your country, or for any nation.

You are neither superior nor inferior to any other human being.

James 4:7; Galatians 6:3; John 8:44

5

Jesus Christ has nailed racism to the Holy Cross on your behalf.

Jesus Christ has redeemed you from condemnation by racists and racism.

Jesus Christ has redeemed you from every injustice, oppression or violence of racism.

God's Holy Word is the most powerful weapon against racism.

Jesus Christ has overcome every form of evil in the world, including racism.

Romans 8:1; Colossians 2:14-15; John 16:33; Romans 5:1-11; Isaiah 61:1-3; Ephesians 6:17-18

6

You have the authority to trample the serpent and scorpion spirit of

racism through Jesus Christ.

God has outlawed racism!

God has never authorized racism!

Racism is ungodly and contrary to the Word of God and will not prevail against you.

Anyone, including racists, who attacks you do so without God's permission and will fail.

Luke 10:18-19; Isaiah 54:15,17; Exodus 3:7; Zechariah 7:10

7

Racism is a sin against God and an offense against humanity.

You are not a "slave" to the sin of racism or to any racist tradition.

You are not subject to the evil spirit of racism and its lies.

The Lord God is your Rock, Fortress, Deliverer and Strength over racism.

The Lord God is your Shield, Horn of Salvation, Stronghold and Refuge against racism.

Romans 6:15-23; Exodus 23:9; Zechariah 7:10; Psalms 27:1; Psalms 31:1-5; Psalms 91:1-2

8

H e, Christ Jesus, your Savior Who is in you, is greater than the

foul spirit of racism.

Racism has no real spiritual power over your life because Christ lives in you.

Racism has no real spiritual authority over your life because Christ lives in you.

So, racism can never crush or destroy you, if you resist it with the truth and power of God's Holy Word.

You have the victory of Jesus Christ over the odious spirit of racism.

Jesus Christ has freed you forever from the condemnation of racism and you are free indeed!

Therefore, racism cannot condemn you!

1 John 4:4, 5:4; 2 Corinthians 4:8-11; Romans 8:1; John 8:32,36

9

Racism may come against you, but you can and must stand against

it with God's Holy Word to overcome it.

Racists may gather and conspire against you; nonetheless, in the awesome Name of Jesus Christ, their plans will never succeed against your life.

Through Jesus Christ, you are more than a conqueror of racism, because He lives in you and is your shield and protection.

Through Jesus Christ, God executes justice for you, because He lives in you.

So, you are a victor in Jesus Christ; therefore, you are a victor and not a victim of racism.

Jeremiah 1:19; Isaiah 54:15; Romans 8:37; Psalms 103:6; Psalms 140:12; Psalms 146:5-7; Deuteronomy 10:18; Zechariah 7:9

10

In Jesus Christ, you are free now and always.

Racism is from the devil, the father of all lies; therefore, there is no truth in racism.

Your body is a temple of God, and racism cannot defile it, unless you allow it.

You possess the complete armor of God (Jesus Christ Himself)—truth of God's Holy Word, the Sword of the Spirit, the Breast Plate of Righteousness, and the Shield of Faith to quench the fiery darts of the vile spirit of racism.

You are covered with the armor of God. So; use and fire God's Holy Word against racism!

John 8:31, 32, 36; John 8:44; 1 Corinthians 3:16; Isaiah 61:1-3; Ephesians 6:10-18

11

*R*acism cannot stand against the righteousness of Jesus Christ in

you.

He Who is in you is greater than racism in the world.

You have the mind of Jesus Christ and have received God's Holy Spirit to deal victoriously with racism.

You have the victory of Jesus Christ over the odious spirit of racism and its nasty outgrowth racism.

1 John 2:1; 1 John 4:4; 1 John 5:4; 1 Corinthians 2:16

12

*J*esus Christ has given you a renewed thought life through God's Holy

Word, to gain victory over racism.

You are equipped with the power of God's Holy Word within you as you battle racism.

Jesus Christ has put racism under your feet. Believe it!

You have the power of your faith against racism. Believe it11 Use it! Apply it!

You have the power and authority of Jesus Christ to trample the serpent and scorpion spirit of racism.

Exercise the power and authority of Christ in you against racism!

Romans 12:2; Hebrews 4:12-13; 1 Corinthians 15:27; Luke 10:17-19

13

*Y*ou are the head over racism and not the tail under it.

Your constant, fervent prayer melts down the foundations of racism.

The power of your holy worship in the secret place of the Most High God, has you under His protection from any evil, including racism.

Racism cannot condemn you because Jesus Christ has freed you from any and all condemnation.

You already have Christ's victory over the vile spirit of racism, its lies and condemnation.

Deuteronomy 28:13; James 5:16; Psalms 91:1-3; Romans 8:1

14

Racism has no power over the peace of God within you unless you give it access to your heart and mind.

Through Jesus Christ, God called me clean, so racism cannot call me unclean or inferior.

God does not show favoritism to anyone; He judges the heart and not appearance.

Racism is an attack on God Himself, who created all of humanity.

Isaiah 26:3-4; Philippians 4:6-7; Acts 10:28-29; Isaiah 54:15; 1 Samuel 16:7

15

*R*acism is wrong and immoral, an offense against humanity, and a

sin against God.

You have God's full armor, so you can withstand the schemes of racism.

God's holy power is in you because you possess the power of Jesus Christ and the Holy Spirit Who dwell within you.

God created you for His glory and He will always glorify Himself in you, despite the racism around you.

Ephesians 6:10-18; Isaiah 43:1-3, 7; Mark 7:8; John 13:31-32

16

You are sanctified through Jesus Christ, and you can do all things

through Him who strengthens you.

With Jesus Christ, racism is an ineffective tool of the demonic spirit of racism against your life.

God has excellent plans for your life. Believe and receive that He has wonderful plans for you!

Racism is an offense and a sin against God the Maker of all races.

The vile spirit of racism is an agent of the devil which comes to steal, kill and destroy your life; but you have Jesus Christ Who has given you life more abundantly.

1 Corinthians 6:11; Philippians 4:13; Jeremiah 29:11; John 10:10

17

*R*acism is an assault on God's excellent Image reflected in people of all races.

Racism is an assault on the human race and your own specific race and ethnicity.

Through Jesus Christ, all of humanity has become one under God.

Racism cannot distort your true image in Jesus Christ; only you can by allowing the lies of racism to pollute your heart and mind.

Galatians 3:26-28; Galatians 5:1; Genesis 1:26-27

18

*B*ecause of Jesus Christ and the Holy Spirit power in you, any racist

plot or attack against you will always fail.

If you trust God, He will always plead your case against the odious spirit of racism and its intrigues.

Racism has no real spiritual power over God's individual purpose for your creation and existence.

It is God (and not any racist) who has the key to your prosperity and peace.

God gives you the power to acquire true wealth and be prosperous in the mighty Name of Jesus Christ!

Jeremiah 1:17-19; Jeremiah 29:11; Deuteronomy 8:18; Psalms 35:1-10; Psalms 35; Isaiah 54:15

19

*G*od's Spiritual light is greater than the perversion of racism.

Racism is a form of spiritual perversion, a product of the devil's kingdom of darkness that lacks God's holy light.

You have the glorious light of God in you that smothers the darkness of racism.

Racism can never overshadow or make obscure the light of the truth of God's Holy Word.

Jesus Christ has overcome racism for you.

God (and not racists or racism) is in charge of your daily life, and He has great plans for your life.

John 3:19; 1 John 1:5; 1 John 5:4; John 16:33; Jeremiah 29:11

20

*G*od's Word is powerful and sharper than a double-edged sword, and

pierces and exposes every hidden thought and motive.

God's Word pierces through the loathsome spirit of prejudice and racism; it exposes racism and its nasty lies, whether hidden or blatant.

God's Holy Spirit intercedes for you against the foul spirit of racism.

God's Holy Word is the (and your) Sword of the Spirit against the odious spirit of racism and its nasty fruit racism.

Hebrews 4:12-13; Romans 8:26-27

21

You must ultimately tackle and overtake racism with God's Word.

You must bind racism with God's Word.

You must thrash racism with God's Word.

You must loose racism to destruction with God's Word.

You must expose and overtake racism with God's Word.

Matthew 18:18-19; Hebrews 4:12-13; Psalms 124:2-5; Ephesians 6:10-18

22

You must veto and eliminate racism with God's Word!

You must rebuke and renounce racism with God's Word!

You must stand against the injustice and oppression of racism with the truth of God's Holy Word!

God knows who you are; you are of Jesus Christ in Him and not of the foul spirit of racism.

Through Jesus Christ, God has justified and redeemed you from the sin of racism.

Isaiah 1:17; Isaiah 54:17; 1 Corinthians 1:30; 1 Corinthians 6:11; Romans 5:1-11; Ephesians 6:10-18; Exodus 3:7; Exodus 23:9; Jeremiah 7:5-7; Zechariah 7:9-10; Galatians 2:16,3:11; Philippians 2:13

23

As you submit to God through Jesus Christ, you can and must resist

the devil and its vile spirit of racism, who will flee from you.

God is for you, so racism cannot be against you—racism cannot defeat you.

God's power rescues you from every evil trap, including the trap of racism that is set for you by racists.

Trust God and believe in His omnipotent, omnipresent and supernatural power over all things, including racism.

James 4:7; Romans 8:31; Psalms 124:2-5; Colossians 1:13-14; Psalms 91:14-15

24

*G*od has thoughts of peace, great hope and a great future for you!

Racism must submit to God's Word.

Jesus Christ is the only way to God; He is the only Mediator between God and you.

Through Jesus Christ, you have gained the power of the truth, authority and promise of God's Holy Word.

Through Jesus Christ, you have daily victoy over racism and the despicable spirit behind it.

Jeremiah 29:11; I Timothy 2:5-6; 1 John 5:4; 2 Corinthians 10:3-6

25

*T*hrough Jesus Christ, you have obtained eternal life.

Racism is from the satanic kingdom of darkness.

But God has delivered you from racism through Jesus Christ.

You do not possess the spirit of fear of racism, but the spirit of courage, power, love and a sound mind to deal victoriously with it.

You possess the victorious power of the Holy Spirit through Jesus Christ to overcome the challenges and obstacles set forth before you by the evil spirit of racism.

Receive God's Holy Spirit and become empowered for victory over the loathsome spirit of racism and its vile activities through its human hosts.

2 Corinthians 6:4-10; 2 Timothy 1:7; Colossians 1:13; John 16:33; 1 John 5:4; Acts 1:8

26

God's grace is sufficient for you to defeat racism and He has raised you

above racism through Jesus Christ.

God always renews your strength; therefore, racism cannot wear you out; racism cannot make you tired or faint.

Jesus Christ has set and made you free; the truth of God's Word has set and made you free; and you are free indeed from the clutches and shackles of racism.

2 Corinthians 12:9; Isaiah 40:31; John 8:31-32,36

27

You possess the spiritual power of Jesus Christ to deal triumphantly with the wiles and intrigues of racism.

Through Jesus Christ, the Holy Spirit of God dwells in you; and through Him Holy Spirit fire power also dwells in you.

In the awesome Name of Jesus Christ, your praise, worship and thanksgiving manifest God's presence and power that defeats racism for you.

John 4:24; John 13:31-32; John 14:15-17; John 15:7-8; 2 Corinthians 2:14-15; 1 Chronicles 29:10-13

28

*G*od is faithful to establish you and guard you from the evil spirit of

racism.

By the power of God through Jesus Christ in you, you can run against any racist forces; you can break down any racist barrier or wall.

You are loaded with God's Holy Word and empowered by His Holy Spirit through Jesus Christ; so, you are God's battleaxe against racism.

God is a just and faithful God; He is a strong Tower for you against racism.

2 Thessalonians 3:3; 2 Samuel 22:30; Proverbs 18:10; Jeremiah 51:20-23

29

God's Word does not change. God's Word stands forever.

And yes, God's Word stands forever against racism.

Racism lacks real power to blind your heart and mind to the good news of the Gospel of Jesus Christ.

Only you can choose to give the spirit of racism access to your heart and mind.

1 Peter 1:25; Isaiah 40:8; Ephesians 4:27

30

God's Word is a lamp onto your feet; it guides you against all evil, including racism.

If you are willing and obedient, God's Holy Word and Holy Spirit will direct and order your steps.

Racism lacks the power to make you walk away from God; only you can choose to do so.

The power of your faith-fueled prayers will compel racism to submit to God's Word.

Psalms 119:105; Psalms 37:23; Joshua 1:7-9; James 4:7

31

The power of your faith-loaded prayers captures and binds racism with

God's Word.

Your powerful prayers thrash racism with God's Word!

The power of the authority of Jesus Christ in you and your faith bind the wicked activities of the foul spirit of racism.

Your prevailing prayers suffocate the activities of the vile spirit of racism with God's Word!

The power of your prayers loose racist activities to destruction with God's Word!

1 Thessalonians 5:17; James 5:16; Matthew 18:18

32

The power of your prayers exposes and overtakes racism with God's

Word.

The power of your prayers vetos and eliminates racism with God's Word.

The power of your prayers rebukes and renounces racism with God's Word.

You must walk worthy before God even as you deal with racism.

1 Thessalonians 5:17; James 5:16; Ephesians 4:1, 12-13; John 8:44

33

You do not have the option to be wicked or cruel, not even toward

racists.

You do not have the option to have a perverse heart, not even toward racists.

You do not have the option to gloat over the demise of anyone, not even that of racists.

You do not have the option to slander, not even a racist person.

Psalms 101:4; Proverbs 11:20; James 4:11; Proverbs 24:17

34

You do not have the option to be vengeful, not even to racists.

You do not have the option not to forgive anyone, not even a racist person.

You are not a casualty of racism; instead, racism will become your casualty.

God has rejected the tradition of racism.

If you are obedient to God's Holy Word, those who perpetrate racism against you oppose God and His Holy Word; and anyone who opposes God is an enemy of God.

Hebrews 10:30; Leviticus 19:18; Matthew 15:3; Mark 11:25; Exodus 23:22

35

You have a renewed spirit in Jesus Christ.

God's Holy Word renews your mind daily; so you should not allow your mind to conform to the tradition of racism in the world.

A superiority complex is self-deceit, a lie of the devil and a sin against God.

You can choose to activate your faith against racism and reject the tradition of racism, of deceipt and lies of racism.

You have the option to choose God's Holy Word or the racist tradition of man. Which option have you chosen?

You have the option to reject racism or to accept it.

Romans 12:2; Galatians 2:20, 6:3; Matthew 21:21-22; John 8:44; 1 Kings 18:21; Matthew 6:24

36

An inferiority complex is a distortion of your mind, a lie of the devil

and a sin that causes self-defeat. Reject it!

Racism cannot condemn you because God has approved you through Jesus Christ.

God has given you a measure of faith for you to activate, nurture and grow by the hearing of His Word.

You have the power and authority of Jesus Christ in you to focus your faith against racism. Use it! Apply it! Fire it against the vile spirit of racism and its nasty outgrowth racism!

Romans 8:1; Romans 12:3; John 8:44; Luke 10:17-19; Ephesians 6:10-18

37

*Y*our activated faith diminishes the power of the odious spirit of racism and ultimately defeats it and its nasty outgrowth racism.

Therefore, there is no need to despise racists; rather despise their actions and their evil, wicked schemes and manipulations.

You are not to loathe racists even as you fight against their racist activities.

God has asked you to love your neighbors as you love yourself, including racists.

You have the choice to obey God's Word and love racists while you rebuke and refute their lies and evil actions, and renounce racism and the foul spirit behind it.

You can choose not to practice evil, even against racists.

Matthew 22:39; 1 Peter 1:7; James 1:3, 12; Matthew 5:43-48

38

*Y*ou can choose to discard all bitterness, wrath, anger, clamor, malice

and evil words, even against racists.

Racists and racism should not make you remain in a state of carnal, unholy anger; rather, they should trigger righteous anger in you and empower you to succeed.

Your fear of racism contradicts the power Jesus Christ in you against racism and the power of your own faith in God's Holy Word.

For you, Jesus Christ has gained ultimate victory over racism.

Believe now and always that through Jesus Christ, you have the ultimate victory over the despicable spirit of racism and its vile product racism.

2 Timothy 1:7; James 1:19-20; Psalms 37:8; Proverbs 14:17,29; Ephesians 4:30-32; Exodus 23:22; John 16:33; 1 John 5:4

39

God is always with you at all times and He will never leave or forsake

you.

God has asked you to be strong and of good courage and not to be afraid of any evil, including racism.

You belong to Jesus Christ, God's only Son, our Lord and Savior Who is God's love, grace and mercy to you and all of humanity. So, you are above racism.

By your own faith in the power of God's Word, His unseen spiritual lightning and silent thunderbolts strike the odious spirit of racism; this foul spirit has been defeated by Jesus Christ on your behalf.

1 Corinthians 6:19-20; Joshua 1:7-9; Galatians 3:26; Ephesians 1:5, 19-23; John 1:12; Psalms 148:8; Psalms 144:6;

40

Righteousness and justice are the foundation of God's holy Throne.

God fires at all evil; and yes, He fires against racism too.

God's unseen holy fire burns up all evil, including racism.

God's warring angels battle and defeat the vile spirit of racim and are victorious over it on your behalf.

By your faith in God's Holy Word, His invisible and invincible army has overrun the loathsome spirit of racism by the precious Blood of Jesus Christ.

Psalms 89:14; Hebrews 12:28-29; Daniel 10:11-15; 2 Kings 6:15-22; Habakkuk 3:19

41

You are a full citizen of the Kingdom of Heaven.

You are a first-class citizen of God's Kingdom.

You are a "majority" and not a "minority" in God's Kingdom.

You are God's child, heir and joint heir with Jesus Christ.

God delivers from evil (including racism) those who love and acknowledge His Name and trust in Him.

Through Jesus Christ, you posses God's Kingdom power within you.

You are a walking power house of God's awesome Word against the vile spirit of racism.

Philippians 3:20; Psalms 37:3-4; Psalms 91:14-15; Romans 8:15-17; Psalms 144:1-2; Titus 3:7

42

Racists call you insignificant but God says you are significant and

He justified, validated and sanctified you through Jesus Christ and racism cannot change this holy truth.

If you obey God's Holy Word, He will plead your cause and oppose those who oppose you.

If you heed to God's Word, your enemies will become God's enemies; racists will become God's adversaries.

God is your Rock and Salvation and racism cannot move you.

Racism opposes you; God's power opposes racism. Racists oppress you and God opposes and demolishes their actions.

Through Jesus Christ, you have God's mantle of victory over racism.

Exodus 23:22; Psalms 18:2; Psalms 27:1-3; Psalms 35; Psalms 62:7; Psalms 125:1; 2 Samuel 22:3; John 8:44; Galatians 6:3; Romans 4:3, 5:1-9; Galatians 2:16, 3:11; 5:22-23; Philippians 2:13

43

Racism is from the kingdom of darkness, and you belong to God's Kingdom of light and truth.

You abide in Jesus Christ and He in you, therefore, you will bear much fruit despite the racism that exists around you.

You possess God's Holy Spirit, Who teaches and guides you to all truth against racism.

Because you a child of the Most High God, redeemed through Jesus Christ, as racists fight you, God fights racists and no mere mortal has ever battled God and won.

Through Jesus Christ, racists and their wicked schemes have been made your footstool.

You have the victory of Jesus Christ over every form of evil, including racism.

Colossians 1:13-14; John 15:1-10; John 16:12-15; Matthew 11:28-30; Matthew 22:44; 1 John 5:4; Psalms 110:1-2

44

Superiority or inferiority complexes are not God's truth nor are they

God's reality; therefore, they should not be your reality either.

The foul spirit of racism offers you either the lying spirit of superiority or inferiority complex. Reject both!

Superiority or inferiority complexes deposited in individuals or groups of people, are lies and illusions of the devil.

God did not make anyone superior or inferior to anyone else.

You can choose not to allow racism to become a burden in your life. Give the burden of racism to Jesus Christ.

Faith in God's Word fuels spiritual victory and births material victory against all lies—including racist lies.

Galatians 6:3; Hebrews 11:1; 1 John 5:4; John 8:44

45

In Christ Jesus, you have the foundation of spiritual courage to battle

racism.

The odious spirit of racism fabricated the lies behind the mindet of superiority and inferiority, and only the ignorant and spiritually complacent are deceived by such lies.

Therefore, racism lacks real power to interfere with your life's potential and achievement; only you can choose to give racists unauthorized, illegal access to your life.

God can give you true spiritual knowledge and wisdom against racism. Read and meditate on His Holy Word.

God's protective power buffers you from the foul spirit of racism.

1 Corinthians 3:11; Revelation 12:10-11; Psalms 37; Psalms 91; Psalms 109; John 8:44; Proverbs 18:10; Isaiah 11:2; Ecclesiastes 7:12; James 1:5

46

*G*od's Holy Word, which is inseparable from Him, is the most important Factor in your life.

Material possessions are important, but should not rule your life.

Material possessions cannot give you authentic spiritual knowledge and wisdom to deal with the odious spirit of racism; all true knowledge and wisdom come from God.

You are not a slave to material possessions; so, do not submit your heart, mind and will to the vile spirit of racism in order to obtain material things.

You should not be a slave to anyone, including racists who may possess more material things than you do.

You should not be a slave to the vile spirit of racism who orchestrates racism.

John 1:1; 2 Timothy 3:16-17; Deuteronomy 8:3; Matthew 4:4; Proverbs 4:6-7; Hebrews 4:12

47

Your individual spiritual success is more important than your material success.

If you prioritize the Triune God, He will prioritize your spiritual prosperity, and then your material success.

God's Holy Spirit dwells in you; the power of God's Holy Word is in you; so, you are a power house of God!

The evil spirit of racism schemes to cause you anger, self-defeat and self-destruction. Don't allow it access to your emotions.

Through Jesus Christ, you have spiritual rule over the evil spirit of racism.

Therefore, racism is a slave to you—you are not a slave to racism.

1 Corinthians 7:20-23; Matthew 6:33; Psalms 49:6-9; 1Timothy 6:17; Romans 6:16-18; Proverbs 15:1; Proverbs 22:24-25; Deuteronomy 6:25; Psalms 1:1-2; John 10:10; Matthew 4:4

48

*F*ear leads to defeat by evil; it can bring you self-defeat and self-

destruction through any form of evil, including racism.

God's Holy Word is the most important resting-place for our spiritual and physical well-being. Read and meditate on it daily and build your faith.

Believing-faith empowers you with spiritual courage to gain victory over any form of evil, including racism.

In the spirit, Jesus Christ has raised you far above the loathsome spirit of racism, and because you have received Christ, you too have His power and authority over this vile spirit.

Now, you are the head over racism and not the tail behind or beneath it.

Joshua 1:7-9; 2 Timothy 1:7; Job 4:14-15; Hebrews 11:1-2; Mark 11:23-24; Hebrews 11:6; Isaiah 26:3, 12; James 1:6; Psalms 127:1; Colossians 2:14-15; Ephesians 1:19-23; Deuteronomy 28:13

49

You belong to God and to no other.

God has chosen you and calls you holy and dearly loved.

God loves you with an everlasting love.

Through Jesus Christ, God has given you the right to become His child.

The vile spirit of racism and its nasty outgrowth racism lack the power and authority to change God's holy truth about who you are in Jesus Christ.

Despite racism, God wants you to prosper in all things and to be in good health, just as your soul prospers.

Romans 8:35-39; Romans 14:7-8; 1 Peter 2:9; Ephesians 1:4-5; Ephesians 2:19

50

Nothing could ever separate you from God's love through Jesus

Christ.

Through Jesus Christ, God has justified you—so you have the righteousness of Christ, and you have peace in and with Him.

You are empowered by God's Holy Spirit and His Holy Word through Jesus Christ; therefore, no weapon formed against you shall prosper in Jesus' Name.

God has given you the righteousness of Jesus Christ.

The awesome power of God's Holy Spirit dwells in you through Jesus Christ. Use that awesome fire power against racism!

Empowered by God's Holy Spirit and Holy Word through Jesus Christ, you have been sanctified—set apart to do great exploits in God's awesome name!

Romans 8:35-39; Isaiah 54:17; Romans 5:1-11; 1 Corinthians 1:30; Romans 3:22

51

*G*od has justified you; therefore, racism cannot and will never condemn

you.

No person, circumstance or situation, including racism, could ever condemn, revile or denounce you, if you know who you are in Jesus Christ.

You are more than a conqueror through Jesus Christ, Who strengthens you.

God is light and there is no darkness in Him. Racism is from the kingdom of darkness, therefore reject it!

You are a child of the light and do not belong to the darkness.

You are child of God and not a child of the abohorrent spirit of racism—reject this foul spirit now and always!

Romans 8:1,37; 1 Thessalonians 5:5; Isaiah 60:1-2; 1 John 1:5; Ephesians 6:12

52

You are Christ's bondservant, pledged to obey Him and absolutely nothing else, not even racism, could ever enslave your mind unless you allow it.

The evil spirit of racism tries to turn you into a defeated spirit—don't allow it!

A defeated spirit is not a conquering spirit.

A defeated spirit lacks authentic spiritual knowledge.

A defeated spirit lacks true self-knowledge.

A defeated spirit has not tapped into the power of God's Holy Word and His Holy Spirit within them.

A defeated spirit is not empowered by God's Holy Word—but you are not a defeated spirit; rather, you are empowered by God's Word amd made victorious by Him through Jesus Christ.

Hosea 4:6; 1 Corinthians 7:22; Romans 8:37; 1 John 5:4

53

A defeated spirit has not activated the conqueror within them through

Jesus Christ.

Only you can choose defeat if you lack faith and trust in God.

Only you can choose victory in Jesus Christ if you have faith and trust in God.

You possess great talents, gifts, ability and potential. Only you can turn your talents, gifts, ability and potential into success, if you choose to partner with the Triune God.

By the power and authority of Christ in you only you can choose to use your talents, and only you can choose to bury your talents.

There is no victory within defeat. There is no victory in racism.

There is everlasting victory in Jesus Christ when you say yes to Him!

Matthew 25:14-30; Luke 1:37; Matthew 19:26; 1 John 5:4

54

*T*he power of God's Holy Spirit is a weapon of mass destruction against racism or any other form of injustice, wickedness, oppression or evil.

God has not authorized any stronghold of racism to control your life.

Jesus Christ has freed you from the stronghold of racism in your life.

Only you can turn defeat into victory, if you believe and trust God, His Holy Word and promises, abide in Christ and He in you, and obey God's Word.

With God, all things are possible for yo for you.

Now, arise and shine for the glory of God has risen upon you to smother the darkness of racism.

Romans 8:2; Micah2, 6:6-8; Deuteronomy 24:17; Isaiah 5:7, 61:1-3; 58:6; 59:15; John 8:32,36; Luke 1:37; Matthew 19:26

55

*O*nly you can allow the stronghold of racism in your life.

Through Jesus Christ, you possess God's armor for victory over the vile spirit of racism.

You have the choice to put on or not put on God's full armor to melt down the foundations of the evil spirit of racism.

Only God has the supernatural power to uproot the vile spirit of racism from the heart and mind of anyone once they submit to the truth of His Holy Word.

Through Jesus Christ, you have God's supernatural power in you to shatter the evil schemes of the foul spirit of racism against your life. Use it! Apply it!

Through Jesus Christ in you, you are empowered by the Holy Spirit Who dwells in you. Therefore, you are more than a conqueror of racism through Christ Who loves you!

Ephesians 6:10-18; James 4:7; Jeremiah 1:10

56

Jesus Christ, you possess God's spiritual armor for daily victory over

the vile spirit of racism—Use it! Apply it!

God's full armor turns you into a spiritual powerhouse that demolishes the intrigues, wicked schemes and evil machinations of the odious spirit of racism.

With God, you can apply spiritual warfare and slay the giant Goliath of racism.

You have the choice to defeat racism or to allow racism to defeat you.

Through Jesus Christ, you are more than a conqueror of the foul spriit of racism.

Ephesians 6:10-18; 1 Samuel 17:40-51; Luke 10:17-19; Romans 8:37

57

God's blueprint for your life remains unchanged even when racism tries

to distort it in your mind.

God's excellent purpose for your life is His divine pathway for your life that racism has no true power over.

The Name of Jesus Christ has the ultimate power over any form of evil, including racism.

Declare the awesome Name of our Lord and Savior Jesus Christ and plead His precious Blood over your life and make the foul spirit of racism tremble and flee from you!

Jeremiah 29:11; Matthew 28:18; Philippians 2:9-11; Romans 14:11; James 2:19

58

Your own faith in God's Word which is inseparable from God Himself, destroys any illusion of power that racism may hold over your life.

With God, racism becomes nothing but a toothless bull, a peon in your daily life.

With God on your side, you are a "David" over the "Goliath" racism.

By your faith in God's Holy Word, the power and authority of Jesus Christ, and the fire power of God's Holy Spirit in you, you can slay the "Goliath" racism.

Stand in and on the victory of Jesus Christ over the vile spirit of racism.

Ephesians 1:13–14; 1 Samuel 17:40-51; John 16:33; Luke 10:18-19; 1 John 5:4

59

*W*hen you fight a just cause with just actions, God is on your side

and victory is yours.

Self-hatred drives hate for others. Self-hatred drives racists to hate others. Self-hatred causes racists to be angry towards others.

The odious spirit of racism fuels anger in racists and in those who are targeted by racists.

There is no victory in anger; so let go of your own anger towards racists. Vengeance belongs to God and not to you.

God does not do business with angry individuals.

God loves justice; let Him be the one to avenge racists on your behalf.

""Vengeance is mine, I will repay", says the Lord." (NKJV)

Hebrews 10:30; Romans 12:19; Colossians 3:8; James 1:20; Zechariah 7:9-10; Proverbs 14:7; Proverbs 29:11, 22

60

*I*f you let God, He will help you to let go of anger so that He can work

with you.

God does not attend "self-pity parties," because His Holy Spirit is a conqueror and not a victim.

If you let God, He will help you get rid of self-pity which is the devil's weapon of defeat against your life.

By the power of God's Word which renews your mind daily, God helps you to end your "self-pity party," and through Jesus Christ, transforms you into more than a conqueror of the challenges or obstacles you face, including racism.

Don't allow the odious spirit of racism to cause you to live in defeat or with unrighteous anger.

Turn your unrighteous anger into righteous anger and fire your faith-fueled prayers, your spiritual warfare against the vile spirit of racism.

Proverbs 20:22; Matthew 11:28-30; Philippians 4:13; 1 Corinthians 10:13; Ephesians 6:10-18

61

*R*ighteous anger is based on God's Holy Word; it is constructive

and stirs our spirit and soul to gear up against racism through spiritual warfare.

Righteous anger is godly anger and causes us not to sin against God.

Righteous anger will not cause us to curse our racist offenders or plot vengeful or
retaliatory schemes against them.

Righteous anger is not a quick and fiery anger that seeks to self-destroy or to
destroy others, but stirs us up to rest upon God's faithfulness and sovereign
power to demolish all evil, including racism.

Righteous anger causes us to pray without ceasing, and take positive, constructive steps and actions within the boundaries of God's holy law against evil like
racism.

**Romans 12:21; Ephesians 4:26-27; Ephesians 4:29-32; 2;
Ephesians 6:10-18; Timothy 2:24**

62

*R*ighteous anger triggers prayer, fasting and meditation on God's

Word.

Righteous anger seeks to hear God's voice, directions and strategies on how to deal with the racism that you face.

Righteous anger gives peace knowing that God's power remains in control of all situations.

Righteous anger gives you enduring strength of Jesus Christ so that you can stand in His victory against the injustice of racism.

Righteous anger will always direct you to God's Holy Word, praise and worship; and by faith, it leads you to stand in Christ's victory by the power of the Holy Spirit in you!

Esther 3:12-15,4:1-3, 7; Psalms 37, 68:1, 142, 143, 144, 145

63

You are created in the excellent Image of God so you should not deny who you are or your heritage from Him through Jesus Christ.

You cannot inherit from the One you deny. If you deny Jesus Christ, you cannot inherit eternal salvation from God.

When you deny who you are, you deny God, in whose excellent Image you are created.

Don't let the foul spirit of racism cause you to deny who you are in Jesus Christ. If you deny Christ, God the Father will deny you.

Don't allow the vile spirit of racism to prevent you from accepting Jesus Christ as your Lord and Savior.

Don't allow the vile spirit of racism to turn you into a hypocritical "born again" believer.

Genesis 1:26-27; Matthew 10:33; 2 Timothy 2:12; Mark 8:38

64

External validation from others is false validation.

As a born again Christian believer, validated through the precious Blood of Jesus Christ and owned by God who has deposited the Holy Spirit in you as His mark of ownership of you, you cannot be thrashed by racism, an unholy and foul spirit.

True validation is spiritual validation through Jesus Christ based on God's Holy Word.

God has validated you through Jesus Christ and the Holy Spirit.

Receive God's living Word, Jesus Christ, and obtain the Holy Spirit; then let your true "inner man" be renewed and empowered by Jesus Christ, the Holy Spirit and the Holy Word.

1 Peter 3:15; Hebrews 10:14; John 17:17-19; Romans 5:1,9; Galatians 2:16, 3:11; 1 Timothy 4:4-5; 1 Corinthians 6:11

65

Jesus Christ paid the highest price for your eternal salvation, and God has validated you through Him.

There is no condemnation in you because you are in Jesus Christ, you do not walk according to your flesh but according to the Spirit.

Condemnation of any person is also self-condemnation. Therefore, in God's holy eyes, racists and racism cannot condemn you; and you cannot condemn anyone.

There is no true self-knowledge or wisdom outside the knowledge of God, Who is your Maker.

True knowledge from God, your Creator, is that no one race is better than any other.

John 3:6-7, 16; Romans 8:1; 1 Peter 3:18; 1 Corinthians 15:3-8; Matthew 5:22-23; Proverbs 1:7; James 3:17; 1 Corinthians 2:1-16; Galatians 3:23-28; Colossians 3:11

66

Self-hatred stems from a lack of authentic spiritual and self-knowledge, which comes from a lack of knowledge of God, in whose perfect Image we exist.

Self-hatred originates from spiritual ignorance of God's Holy Word and external abuse of your soul and inner person.

Self-hatred silently builds an invisible and destructive fortress that keeps a person bound in a constant, negative stronghold.

Reject, rebuke, renounce and thrash self-hatred!

Reject racism that tries to deposit self-hatred in your heart and defile your heart!

Hosea 4:6; Romans 8:1; 1 Corinthians 3:16-17; 2 Corinthians 4:3-4; Proverbs 4:23

67

A lack of godly wisdom blinds your heart and mind and leads you down

self-destructive paths and ways.

You are God's beautiful workmanship, and feelings of low-self esteem and un- worthiness are not a handiwork of God.

Don't allow the odious spirit of racism to incarcerate your mind and cause you to develop low self-esteem and a mindset of self-limitations and self- incarceration.

Self-incarceration is locking up your mind and shutting off any or all possibili- ties of advancement and achievement.

Feelings of low self-esteem originate from the devil, the enemy of your soul, and you should reject it.

Hosea 4:6; Proverbs 14:8; Ephesians 2:10; Galatians 5:1

68

*T*he foul spirit of racism can inplant negative thoughts in your mind

and sway you from having a positive mindset. Reject the foul spirit of racism and its lies!

When you are bound by self-hatred, you become bound by self-limitations through the negative power of your own mind. Renounce and veto self-hatred!

True spiritual awareness will give you authentic self-knowledge, which will reveal to you the insecure state of prejudiced or racist individuals.

Carnal insecurity breeds fear and superiority complex in racists, and can inject fear and inferiority complex into the souls of those targeted by racists, if they allow it—so reject it!

Illuminating knowledge from God's Holy Word validates that no one is either superior or inferior to anyone else.

Philippians 4:8-9; 1 Peter 5:8; Romans 12:2-3; Ephesians 4:21-24

69

*S*elf" is the whole entity of "you" that encompasses your spirit, soul

and body, which are created by God.

As a born again believer your spirit is renewed in Jesus Christ; your old "inner man" has been crucified in Him and you are a brand "new man" in Him.

Yes, the foul spirit of racism is not authorized to dwell in you. The odious spirit of racism is not authorized to control or dominate your new man in Jesus Christ.

Through Jesus Christ, God's Holy Spirit is the only Spirit authorized by God to dwell in you; every other contrary spirit is not authorized to dwell in you.

The Spirit of God helps us to activate and power our inherent measure of faith, and drive our creativity through the "superconscious" locus (core) of our spirit.

1 Thessalonians 5:23; John 14:16-17; Romans 8:27; John 16:13; Romans 6:5-14; Galatians 2:20

70

*T*hrough Jesus Christ, God makes you larger than racism.

Spiritual knowledge gives you authenic knowledge about your true identity and nature in Jesus Christ, and this is a silent gear that pushes against the odious spirit of racism until it is permanently stalled and unable to attack or erode your psyche or soul.

Heavenly knowledge is also your spiritual wisdom for mental resistance against racism and its evils.

Receive the fire power of God's Holy Spirit through Jesus Christ—and reject, rebuke, renounce, veto and thrash the loathsome spirit of racism!

Submit to God's Holy Word, resist the evil spirit of racism and it will flee from you!

By the power of Jesus Christ in you, rebuke and calm the tempest storm of racism against your life.

1 John 4:4; 1 John 5:4; Matthew 16:14-17; Proverbs 24:13-14; James 4:7; Mark 4:35-41

108

71

By faith, you are justified before God by the imputed righteousness of

Jesus Christ, and sanctified by God's holy truth—His awesome Word, and through prayer, worship and holy living.

Through Jesus Christ, you have been sanctified—consecreated to do great exploits for God.

Your mind is renewed daily by God's Holy Word; therefore you have mental resistance empowered by God's Word.

Mental resistance is most effective against racism when your human heart and mind are fortified with the power of God through knowledge of His Word.

True self-knowledge is deeply founded in the knowledge of God, Who is the fountain and source of all true knowledge.

Proverbs 1:7; Proverbs 4:5-7; Proverbs 9:10; James 1:5; 1 Corinthians 1:21; John 15:1-17; Jeremiah 29:11

72

Your true self is the real you in Jesus Christ that is embedded in your spiritual purpose and journey as God designed for your life.

Knowing God and understanding our spiritual nature in Jesus Christ, is the gateway to knowing God's purpose for our individual life.

God's grace, our Lord and Savior Jesus Christ, is more than sufficient for each of us to gain individual and collective victory over racism. Receive Him in your heart!

You must exercise positive spiritual dominance over racism through spiritual warfare before you can ever see actual victory in your physical environment.

God's spiritual truth and understanding take human folly out of carnal ignorance in dealing with racism. Receive, believe and embrace it!

2 Corinthians 12:9; Luke 10:18-19; Ephesians 6:10-18; 1 Corinthians 3:19; 1 Corinthians 1:20

73

*F*or the power of God against racism to work on your behalf, you must

believe it, embrace it and activate the measure of faith in you.

Racism cannot stand against the Holy Word of God.

Racism is no match against the holy anointing fire power of God.

The key to the mantle of spiritual victory over racism lies within you.

You have the awesome power of Jesus Christ and the Holy Spirit in you!

Romans 12:3; Hebrews 11:6; Romans 8:31; 1 John 4:4; 1 John 5:4; Hebrews 4:12-13; Ephesians 6:10-18

74

You are made in the excellent Image of an awesome God, and through Jesus Christ, you have become a child of God.

Your spirit reflected in your racial and ethnic makeup is special, unique and beautiful, and is created by God in His excellent image.

By accepting Jesus Christ into your life, you have received God's Holy Spirit.

He, Jesus Christ, who is in you, is greater than the despicable spirit of racism and its nasty fruit racism.

The vile spirit of racism lacks legitimate authority and power to accuse you of anything—because He (Christ) has cancelled all charges against you.

Genesis 1:26-27; Galatians 3:26; John 1:12; 1 John 3:2; Colossians 2:14-15; John 14:16-17

75

he real "You" comes from your spirit that belongs to God and has

been redeemed by Jesus Christ.

The real "You" now has access to God through Jesus Christ and is fortified by the power of the Holy Spirit of God that dwells within you.

You are not illegitimate; Jesus Christ has made you legitimate.

You have been justified—made righteous, holy and blameless through Jesus Christ.

You have been sanctified—set apart for God's divine work and continually being conformed to the image of Jesus Christ.

To become sanctified, you must submit to God's Holy Word and will, resist sin, seek holiness and prioritize the spiritual things.

Ephesians 1:7-8; Revelation 12:11; Hebrews 9:12-14; John 14:6; 1 Peter 2:4; 1 John 3:2; Galatians 2:16, 3:11, 3:23, 4:7; Romans 4:3, 5:1,9; Philippians 2:13

76

God has given you many million-dollar talents and gifts.

You are a special person with a unique God purpose in life.

You are not a mishap, coincidence, mistake or shame.

You are a blessing to yourself, family, friends and co-workers.

You are a blessing to your neighborhood and community.

You are a blessing to your city, county, district, state, country and the world.

You are a blessing to your enemies.

You are a blessing to even racists, and others who have also offended and hurt you in any manner.

Matthew 25:14-30; Luke 19:12-28; Jeremiah 29:11; Jeremiah 1:5; Genesis 12:1-4; Ezekiel 34:26

77

God's divine favor within you is enough for your spiritual and material

success.

God has already blessed you with spiritual gifts, talents and great potential.

The actions of a prejudiced person lack the ultimate power to stop you from achieving your success, unless you permit them.

God has thoughts of peace and not of evil, to give you excellent hope and future.

You are always beautiful in the eyes of God your Creator.

Ephesians 1:18-23; Psalms 23:5; Jeremiah 1:19, 29:11; Isaiah 54:15

78

*Y*ou made in the excellent Image of the Triune God.

You are born equal in dignity and humanity to every other person.

Your spiritual gifts and talents, when utilized properly, effectively and efficiently through the guidance of God's Holy Spirit, will make you highly successful.

You are elegant in the eyes of all of God's worthy creations.

You are a special being with a unique purpose in life.

Ask God's Holy Spirit in you to help you identify God's purpose for your life.

Genesis 1:26-27; Matthew 25:14-30; Luke 19:12-28; Jeremiah 29:11; Jeremiah 1:5; 1 Timothy 4:4-5

79

*F*or your faith to move into spiritual action, you must activate it by the

power of the Word of God by first accepting Jesus Christ as your Lord, Savior and Redeemer.

Your unwavering faith:
Is the solid foundation of your relationship with God.
Means believing and understanding that with God, all things are possible.
Means believing God, His Holy Word, and having all confidence and trust in Him at all times—even when He doesn't seem to make sense to you.
Also means believing God and trusting His will, even when His will seems to contradict yours.
Is trusting God even when your prayers seem to go unanswered.

James 2:20; Hebrews 11:1, 6; Mark 11:23; Luke 1:37; Matthew 19:26

80

*G*od's Holy Word empowers and fine tunes your faith, that is, it fuels

your faith to precise spiritual effectiveness.

Your faith in God divinely focuses your spirit, mind, emotions, will, thoughts and actions against racism.

For every step of faith in God through Jesus Christ, a journey of success begins.

God's powerful guiding spiritual light takes you from the paths of oppression and injustice to freedom and justice.

Don't allow the vile spirit of racism and its willing human hosts (racists) to dampen your faith in God's supernatural power to destroy their wicked activities against your life.

Always—focus your faith against racism!

Psalms 119:105; Matthew 17:20; Luke 17:6; 2 Corinthians 4:6; Isaiah 60:19; Psalms 18:28; Psalms 37; Jeremiah 1:19; Isaiah 54:15, 17

81

*W*hen the light of God shines in and on you daily, neither racism

nor its evils will be able to darken His paths of triumph for you.

God's Holy Word empowers you to fine-focus your faith against racism.

Focusing your faith against racism is only possible by hearing and meditating on God's Word.

Your activated faith is a godly giant against racism—Apply it!

1 John 1:5; Hebrews 4:12-13; Colossians 1:13-14; Romans 10:17; Joshua 1:7-9

82

*G*od's Word reminds you to journey through the rugged challenges and

obstacles of life by faith and not by sight.

Fear will exclude faith and invite unbelief into your heart and mind.

For God to move on your behalf against racism, you must have the faith to believe that He can—and He will.

When God's Word is the truth you receive and believe, and you have 100% trust and confidence in Him—He becomes your refuge and fortress, the only One in Whom you trust and put your hope in.

2 Corinthians 5:7; 1 John 4:18; Psalms 23:4, 91:1-4; Hebrews 11:6

83

Your faith must be bigger than racism around you in order for your individual victory to become reality.

Faith works from within your heart, and so your inward person must be in complete control of your outward person in order for you to control your physical surroundings.

Unless you believe that the power of Jesus Christ in you is greater than racism, you will continue to see yourself as a victor over racism; rather than a victim of racism.

Through Jesus Christ, God has already declared you a victor over the vile spirit of racism and its nasty fruit of racism. Believe that you are a victor!

1 John 4:4; 1 John 5:4; Deuteronomy 31:6; Isaiah 41:10; Psalms 112:6-8; Hebrews 10:35-38; Isaiah 26:3-4

84

You have the authority given to you through Jesus Christ to bind racism on Earth and therefore to bind it in heaven.

You have the authority given to you through Jesus Christ to loose God's power against racism on Earth and in Heaven.

You possess the authority and power of Jesus Christ in you—God's Kingdom power within you to trample on the serpent and scorpion spirit of racism that comes against your life. Use it! Apply it!—in the Name of Christ.

If you trust God, His Holy Word, He will rise up and destroy the wicked activities of your racist enemies.

Child of the Most High God, you are loaded with the awesome power of God through Christ to defeat the foul spirit of racism. Apply it against racism!

Matthew 18:18, 28:18; Luke 10:17-19; Psalms 68:1; Deuteronomy 33:27

85

*T*he Word of God powers your built-in faith, and your faith fortifies

your spirit, which in turn drives your soul and body.

According to your faith, no mountain is too high for God to tear down. No form of racism is too intricate for God to untangle, expose or destroy.

Faith is the foundation of your spiritual, mental and physical courage.

By your faith you are able to fire God's Word against the vile spirit of racism and defeat its evil activities manifested against your life through its racist human hosts.

Your faith in the Name of Jesus Christ ignites the power of God's Holy Word in you.

Romans 10:17; Genesis 18:14; Jeremiah 32:27; Ephesians 4:12-13; Isaiah 54:17

86

*F*aith defeats the seeds of fear, anxiety, anger, frustration, hate, venge-

ance and all other negative emotions, thoughts, actions and words.

God will release you from the oppression of racism by your activated faith in His Holy Word, power, might and glory.

God responds to your faith; so fear not the "Egyptians, racist oppressors who are attacking you, for the "Egyptians" you see today, you shall see no more,

Fear not! Stand firm! You will surely see the salvation of the Lord!

Mark 11:23; John 7:38; John 11:40; Exodus 3:7, 14:13-14; Acts 7:34; Proverbs 3:5-6; Ephesians 1:18-23

87

*G*od must always be your number-one priority in your life.

Seek first the Kingdom of God and His righteousness and everything else that you desire, according to His holy will for your life, you shall receive.

The Kingdom of God is the sovereign and righteous rule of God, where His power, goodness, faithfulness, mercy and judgment reign.

God's kingdom is indestructible. God's kingdom was, is and will continue to be through eternity.

As a child of God who has received Jesus Christ as your Lord and Savior and the power of God's Holy Spirit in you, the Kingdom of God dwells within you.

Believe the truth—God's Kingdom power in you through Jesus Christ is greater than the loathsome spirit of racism.

Matthew 6:33; Luke 10:27; Luke 12:31, 17:20-21; Luke 17:21; 1 Corinthians 4:20

88

*G*od created people of every race, ethnicity and nationality, and He loves

all of humanity.

Regardless of anyone's ethnicity, race or nationality, God's presence and power will come forth within anyone who accepts Jesus Christ—you receive the power the Holy Spirit.

Become a doer of God's Holy Word—live a life of obedience to His Word.

Regardless of anyone's ethnicity, race or nationality, God's presence and power will not appear within anyone who rebels against God, anyone who is living in disobedience to His Holy Word or in deliberate spiritual blindness.

John 3:6-7; John 3:16; Acts 2:1-4; John 7:38; Acts 8:14-17

89

*E*vil such as racism may oppose you but can never conquer God's su-

preme Kingdom power in your life.

The Kingdom of God in you can never be destroyed by anything including the foul spirit of racism.

The Kingdom of God creates a spiritual "giant" within you.

God's Kingdom within you establishes His spiritual power within you through Jesus Christ; and this power becomes the consuming fire of the adversities that you face.

God's consuming fire burns up the wicked activities of the evil spirit of racism on your behalf!

Daniel 2:44; Luke 1:33; Luke 17:20-21; Hebrews 12:28-29

90

You must continue to walk in obedience of God's holy commands, offering forgiveness within your heart to those who offend you.

The spiritual power for you within the promises of the Kingdom of God has no limitations except for the limitations imposed by your lack of faith, unbelief, unforgiveness and disobedience of God's Word.

You are a child of the Most High God—you are justified, sanctified and validated through Jesus Christ; therefore, the despicable spirit of racism cannot defeat you unless you let go of God's Word and His awesome power in you.

Luke 1:33; Ephesians 4:1; Hebrews 11:6; Joshua 1:7-9; Matthew 6:14-1

91

*T*o hold onto God's Word and His promises when you are in the deep-

est valleys of trials and tribulations is your preparation to receive the miracles of the promises of His Word, which never fails.

Do not fear the trials and tribulations of racism because Jesus Christ has overcome it on your behalf.

Fear is not of God, but of the devil, the prince of darkness.

You are born of God through Jesus Christ; therefore you too have overcome the world by your faith in Him.

God's Word is eternal and stands forever; God's Word against racism stands forever!

Psalms 23; 1 John 4:18; 2 Timothy 1:7; John 16:33; Jeremiah 51:20-23

92

*F*ear is the devil's weapon that is designed to cripple your faith and

hold you under carnal bondage.

Fear blinds your spiritual wisdom and fills your mind with lies and distortions about what the evil power of any human or negative spirit can accomplish in your life.

As a born again believer, you have received the authority and power of Jesus Christ in you to trample on the serpent and scorpion spirit of racism. Use it! Apply it against racism—in the mighty Name of Jesus Christ!

You are loaded with God's Holy Word, transformed into God's battleaxe against the vile spirit of racism!

2 Timothy 1:7; John 8:44; Lamentations 3:57; Luke 10:18-19; Jeremiah 51:20-23

93

*T*he spirit of fear is a weapon of defeat and destruction, and bondage of

the mind.

God has not given you a spirit of fear, but of love, power and a sound mind.

Fear also fuels the power that sustains racism against others.

To confront real or imagined fear, you need spiritual courage.

Immerse your heart and mind in God's Holy Word and receive His spiritual courage.

John 8:44; 2 Timothy 1:7; Psalms 23:4; Isaiah 41:13; Joshua 1:7-9

94

*W*hen you fear humans, who are merely creations of God, you fail

to revere the protective, limitless and boundless power of God, the Maker of all humans.

You are to fear only God by revering His power and glory, and do not allow your fear of any man, woman or circumstance to control your life.

Do not allow your fear of racism to control your heart, mind, thoughts, emotions, will or resolve.

Faith overcomes fear—always!

Your faith in God's Holy Word can and will defeat the illegitimate power of the odious spirit of racism against your life.

Psalms 37; Psalms 111:10a; 1 Peter 3:14; Revelations 15:4; Psalms 27:1,3

95

ear can be confronted as you are armed with spiritual courage and

with the Word of God as your ammunition.

To master control of fear is not to destroy it, but to hold every fearful thought captive with the Word and promises of God.

Believe the truth that God's Holy Word has supernatural dominance over all evil, including the vile spirit of racism.

So, reject fear—always!

Grow your faith with God's Holy Word.

Faith smothers fear—always!

2 Corinthians 10:2-5; 2 Timothy 1:7; Isaiah 54:4a; Romans 10:17

96

N o fearful thought that is bound or held captive by the Word

of God with complete and unwavering faith will ever become victorious in your life.

Fear diminishes your faith and transforms it into a double-mindedness that is ineffective in the spiritual realm.

Your faith in God through Jesus Christ frustrates the evil activities of the vile spirit of racism and its willing human recruits.

By your faith in Christ, God's Living Word, the impossible becomes possible in your life.

2 Corinthians 10:2-5; James 1:8; James 4:8; Luke 1:37; Matthew 19:26

97

*F*ear smothers the power of God's spiritual warfare in our lives, be-

cause God responds primarily to our faith.

Your faith must completely replace your fear, for if not, fear will steal your rays of victory from God.

Fear breeds feelings of frustration and accomplishes nothing for you.

Fear, not faith, causes racism to seem like a winning giant against your life.

Exercise your faith against the "giant" racism, like Caleb and Joshua did when they believed God and refused to fear the "giants" they saw.

The power of your faith in God and His Holy Word, cause you to see racism as the "peon" that it is against your life.

Hebrews 11:6; Isaiah 41:10; Isaiah 43:1; Numbers 13:30-33

98

Your faith dispels fear, because the Word and promises of God

within your heart and mind fortify your faith.

It is not an act of faith but an act of fear to believe that the power of any man to do evil against you is greater than the power of God to overcome that evil with good in your life.

Never believe that racism has greater power over your life than God—this is a lie of Satan—don't fall for it!

Believe the truth that God's power is in you through Jesus Christ; He, Christ in you is greater than the despicable spirit of racism.

Romans 8:28,10:17; 1 John 4:4; 1 John 5:4; John 16:33; Isaiah 51:12; 1 Peter 5:8-9; John 8:44

99

To claim God's rays of victory within you, fear must be replaced by

faith.

Faith generates hope, and hope gives rise to patience and sustains your journey into the future, giving rise to God's miracles in your life daily.

Ask God's Holy Spirit to direct your response to racism—then apply the Holy-Spirit directed winning strategies against racism.

Forgiveness does not condone the actions of the person who has committed an offense against you.

Forgive your racist attackers and others who have offended you—hand them over to God's holy and impartial judgement.

Mark 11:25-26; Luke 6:37; I John 4:4; Psalms 38:15; Psalms 71:14; Psalms 78:7; Psalms 119:147; Hebrews 4:12-13

100

*T*he act of forgiveness is a necessary spiritual cleansing for claiming

God's rays of victory over the challenges that you face in your life.

God has asked you to forgive those who offend you just as He forgives your own offenses.

God expects you to forgive your racist attackers and others who offend you on a daily basis.

Forgivess cleanses your heart to receive God's blessings for your life.

Don't allow the evil spirit of racism and its willing human hosts (racists) to seed unforgiveness in your heart.

Always—reject the vile spirit of racism and its wicked activities against any-one!

Mark 11:25-26; Matthew 6:12, 18:21-22

101

The act of forgiveness itself is an act of your will. You have to make the decision to forgive because God has asked you to do so, and as such, it is in your best interest to do so.

Jesus Christ taught us that as believers in Him, when praying, we must first remember to forgive all those who have offended us, even when they are unrepentant.

Do not relent on resisting racism; do not relent on applying spiritual warfare against racism; do not relent on forgiving your racist attackers and other who offend you.

Mark 11:25-26; Matthew 6:12

102

If you wish your own daily offenses to be forgiven by God, you, too,

must forgive daily those who offend you.

Forgive your racist offenders.

For you to be able to offer forgiveness, your heart has to be willing to do so as well.

Truth and mercy are godly paths to justice, and this must include offering forgiveness to racists.

Mark 11:25-26; Matthew 6:12

103

*T*rue and complete forgiveness requires the enabling grace of God and

the intervening power of His Holy Spirit, Who dwells within you.

When you forgive an unrepentant individual who lacked regard for your humanity and did not care about pain that they caused you, you have not absolved them of God's penalty for their sin.

Let go of all unrighteous anger, wrath and malice against your racist attackers, and let God be their impartial Judge.

Mark 11:25-26; Matthew 6:12; Hebrews 4:12-13

104

*Y*ou can learn true forgiveness not necessarily from those who preach

it, but from everyday folks who live and walk in it.

When you forgive an individual of offenses that they commit against you, you free your own spirit and soul to receive God's awesome rays of victory for your life's success.

Make a commitment today to forgive your racist attackers and others who offend you daily.

Let the soil of your heart be cleansed by the power of forgiveness.

Mark 11:25-26; Matthew 6:12

105

*O*nly God has the power to absolve anyone of their sins and the penalty

for their sins through the precious Blood of Jesus Christ; but surely, you can forgive an offense against you.

For every individual that you forgive, you vest into your blessings from God.

Even though God sees racist actions as unjust, oppressive and sinful, He still asks you to forgive all prejudiced and racist individuals.

God is just and He expects and demands justice for all.

God executes justice for the oppressed and delivers justice to the oppressor.

Be assured that God will execute justice for those oppressed by racists; He will surely deliver the oppressed from oppression, wickedness and injustice of racism, and deliver justice to racists!

Mark 11:25-26; Deuteronomy 15:11-15; Deuteronomy 16:11-12; Amos 5:24; Psalms 103:6

143

106

*P*ray for your enemies, those who hate and despise you, those who look

down on you, those who disrespect or disregard you, those who call you inferior, and those who call you nobody and insignificant.

Pray for racists and ask God to beam His spiritual light into them and raise their minds from their carnal state of ignorance to God's enlightening wisdom of true knowledge.

God really loves you and wants your life to be a marvelous success and would never let any evil act, including any form of racism, stand in the way of your success; if you trust Him and His Holy Word in the Name of Jesus Christ.

Let God's Holy Word illuminate your heart and mind daily and be a lamp onto your feet—and smother the darkness of racism.

Matthew 5:44; Luke 6:27-36; Psalms 119:105; Hosea 4:6; James 1:5

107

*W*hen you are blinded spiritually, you cannot see the glory of God's

Kingdom power within you.

Spiritual blindness makes you spiritually impotent and unable to live as an overcomer through Christ Jesus.

Racists are spiritually blind and this is why they are carnally arrogant.

If you deal with the challenges of racism with spiritual blindness, it will defeat you in every manner.

Ask God for a rhema word—spoken word from God on how to deal with a racist situation!

Receive a deeper revelation of God's Holy Word, spoken to you through His Holy Spirit, and become empowered for victory over racism!

Romans 8:5-6; Hosea 4:6; 1 Corinthians 2:9-16; John 6:63; John 10:27

108

If you let God give you His spiritual vision by His Holy Spirit, He will take you to great heights above racism, and He guarantees to give you spiritual and material victory over racism.

With thanksgiving, in prayer and worship, call unto God and He will show you great and mighty things that you do not know.

God's Holy Word illuminates your mind with understanding, wisdom and knowledge, on how to tackle the problem of racism.

Ask God to give you divine winning wisdom to deal victoriously with racism.

Colossians 1:9; Isaiah 11:2; Proverbs 2:6; Proverbs 4:6-7; Proverbs 24:4; Deuteronomy 28:13; Jeremiah 33:3; James 1:5

109

If you ask God to do so, He can flood your spirit with His victorious

beams of light.

Receive God's power hidden in His glorious beams of light radiating from His hand.

The power of God resides within you in the Person of the Holy Spirit and has given you the power to conquer all things through Jesus Christ, including racism in the workplace or elsewhere.

As a born again believer in Jesus Christ, you are spiritually positioned in Him to overcome every racist plot, intrigue or scheme that is fashioned against your life.

Romans 8:37; 2 Corinthians 4:6; John 14:16-17; Acts 1:8; Habakkuk 3:4; Isaiah 54:17

110

*Y*ou are made in the excellent Image of God and you are a special

person with a unique purpose in life.

By the authority and power of Jesus Christ in you, you can trample upon the scorpion and serpent spirit of racism.

Jesus Christ and the Holy Spirit—His Kingdom power within you, are above any evil spiritual force or manifestation in this world and can overcome any adversity, including racism.

He, Christ, Who lives in you is greater that racism that exists around you.

Genesis 1:26-27; Luke 10:18-19; Ephesians 2:4-7; Jeremiah 29:11; 1 John 4:4

111

As a child of God, racism in the workplace lacks real spiritual power to

destroy your career or success in life—unless you believe the lie that it has power over your life.

In accordance with God's Word, every man will reap what he sows, and as such, neither vengeance nor malice is yours to execute against racists.

All things will work out for your good because you love God and are called according to His purpose.

You have the power and authority of Jesus Christ to make the vile spirit of racism and its nasty outgrowth racism your footstool.

Deuteronomy 8:15, 28:14; Romans 8:28; Jeremiah 29:11; Galatians 6:7-8; Hebrews 4:12-13; Psalms 110:1

112

*T*he perpetrators of racism in your workplace or elsewhere are the ulti-

mate victims, because they will never know what it is truly like to open their hearts and positive actions to all of humankind.

Racists have been blinded by the enemy to our soul, the devil, to the the truth of the Gospel of Jesus Christ.

You can conquer racism anywhere with the awesome power and guidance of God's Holy Word and Holy Spirit, in the mighty Name of Jesus Christ.

Through Jesus Christ, you are the "head" over racism and not the "tail" be-neath.

Romans 8:37; Deuteronomy 28:13; 1 Corinthians 1:18; 2 Corinthians 2:15

113

*D*espite racism, you can accomplish your dreams and aspirations.

God has placed no limitations on you and no human being is authorized by God to limit you.

Racism lacks the ultimate power to interfere with God's wonderful will and purpose for your life.

Racists are not authorized by God to attack you and they will fail in their attempt to attack and destroy you, when you trust God in the Name of Jesus Christ.

Jeremiah 29:11; Proverbs 18:21; Isaiah 54:15; Jeremiah 1:19; Psalms 23:5; Isaiah 54:15; Psalms 37:1-11

114

*G*od can illuminate your mind by the power of His Holy Spirit on any

lingering hurt caused by racism—and can begin a healing process within you.

Through Jesus Christ, God can and will heal your hurt, anger and pain from
your experiences with racism, if you submit your will to His, and trust Him
and believe His Holy Word.

Through Jesus Christ receive a renewed spirit and through the Word you receive
a renewed mind.

Renew your heart and mind daily with God's Holy Word, and receive a willing heart that is able and ready to forgive racists and anyone who has hurt you.

When and where there is true forgiveness, the journey of restoration and hope
begins. Start yours today!

John 16:12-15; John 14:25-26; Isaiah 61:1; Psalms 119:105

115

You are a beautiful creation of God, with a spirit that has been illuminated by God's Holy Word and His Holy Spirit, Who dwells within you.

Yes, you can do all things through Jesus Christ, Who strengthens you.

Yes, you are more than a conqueror of racism through Jesus Christ.

Yes, you have the awesome power of God in you through Jesus Christ and can overcome the odious spirit of racism and its nasty outgrowth racism.

Genesis 1:26-27; Romans 8:37; Philippians 4:13

116

*G*od is the Chief Executive Officer of the universe, the world and the

company or establishment where you work.

So, God is your ultimate employer and is above all things and He will judge fairly your claim of racism in the workplace or elsewhere.

God's Holy Word is pure and incorruptible, and regardless of ethnicity, race or nationality, He protects and shields everyone who puts his or her trust in Him.

God hears your earnest prayers and will answer them in accordance with His perfect will and purpose for your life.

1 Peter 1:23-25; Isaiah 26:3-4; Acts 10:34-35; Psalms 91:14-15

117

*G*od will reward you for your excellent hard work even if humans fail to

do so.

If a racist employer "A" refuses to promote or reward your earnest hard work, God will either remove the person(s) who is impeding your career; or He will move you to employer "B" where He has placed someone to reward and promote you; or He will help you establish your own company where you will treat your own employees right.

God is more than excellent in all things, and you also must always strive for excellence in all that you do.

You shall continue to give thanks to God for all things and in all situations.

Ephesians 6:5-8; Matthew 5:16; 2 Timothy 3:16-17; 1 Thessalonians 5:16-18; Psalms 107:1; Psalms 75:5-6

118

*T*hrough Jesus Christ, your spirit is above the vile spirit of racism.

Pray! Pray! Pray without ceasing!

Your prayer with your sustained faith causes the power and glory of God to come forth in your life and on your behalf against life's adversities and challenges, including racism.

Prayer brings forth good tidings into physical manifestation.

Faith fueled prayers of a born again believer births miracles.

Ephesians 2:4-6; 1 Thessalonians 5:17; Romans 4:17; Daniel 10:12-13; James 5:16

119

*R*acism is not your battle but the Lord's.

Jesus Christ has permanently cast down the devil, the enemy of your soul, so He has cast down its demon spirit of racism.

The power of God's Holy Word through Jesus Christ transforms your carnal mind into a spiritual mind that can resist and overcome any and all forms of evil, including racism.

Through your faith in Jesus Christ, you have His victory over the world—over racism!

2 Chronicles 20:15; Revelation 12:10; Romans 12:2

120

*R*acism is a form of injustice, repression and oppression and is contrary to God's Word and His purpose for your life and that of all humanity.

The diversity of races was designed by God to bring a variety of people, male and female alike, all under the banner of the precious Blood of Jesus Christ.

Reject racism because it is an ungodly, divisive factor.

To receive the spirit of racism is to reject God's Holy Word.

To practice racism is to disobey God's Holy Word.

To reject the spirit of racism is to uphold God's Holy Word.

Acts 10:24-29; Galatians 3:26-29; Amos 5:22-24

121

Your daily spiritual relationship with God is far more important than any job or task that you have to accomplish.

Focus on God's power and His limitless possibilities in your life and you will soar like an eagle beyond the limitations that your immediate environment has placed on you.

Always exercise faith in the power of God and in your own God-given abilities.

If you seek God first and His righteousness He will give you victory over racism.

James 4:8; Psalms 18:13-50; Romans 8:37; Matthew 6:33; Jeremiah 29:11

122

*Y*our future lies in the hands of God and not in the hands of any

mere mortal human, such as a racist or any other person.

As you master spiritual victory over racism, become a mentor to another person, teaching them how to become encouraged through reading and meditating on God's Holy Word.

As an ambassor of Jesus Christ, teach and show others how to apply God's Word against racism through Christ.

Believe always in yourself, what you can do and the talents that God has endowed you with, despite racism that exists around you.

Racism is not a legitimate excuse to bury your talents; rather racism should make you want to be highly successful.

Jeremiah 29:11; 2 Corinthians 5:20; Matthew 25:14-30; Psalms 31:15

123

Always expect the best from you and for yourself.

You are clothed in God's full armor for victory over evil, including racism.

Your continuous, powerful, effective, fervent and faith-fueled prayer has power over racism.

You have the victory and authority of Jesus Christ over any form of evil; so you have the ultimate victory over racism.

Invest your God-given talents well—and watch prosperity manifest in your life!

Ephesians 6:10-18; James 5:16; 1 John 5:4; John 16:33; Matthew 28:18

124

*Y*ou can pray to dismantle the illegal trespass of racism over your

life.

Never accept the lies of the vile spirit of racism!

You have the armor of God to overcome the odious spirit of racism.

You can pray without ceasing against the evil spirit of racism.

You can continually declare your victory over racism, as you stand in the victory of Jesus Christ over it.

Your faith fueled prayers dismantles the stranglehold of racism on your life.

1 John 5:4; John 16:33; 1 Thessalonians 5:17; Isaiah 54:17; James 5:16

125

You are a worshipper and the power of holy worship dwells within you through Jesus Christ.

You are created by God to worship Him in truth and in spirit.

In the Name of Jesus Christ, you are empowered by the Holy Spirit to be a worshiper.

The power of your holy worship will expose the wicked activities set up by the obnoxious spirit of racism through its willing and racist human hosts.

The power of your holy worship will break down the walls of injustice.

The power of your holy worship will suffocate and silence the foul spirit of racism.

John 4:23-24; Ephesians 6:16-18; Acts 16:25-26; Hebrews 4:12-13

126

The foul spirit of racism lacks the power to break your daily true communion with God through Jesus Christ; only you can allow it.

Your holy worship is your defensive and offensive weapon against racism.

Your holy worship unshackles you from the demonic chains of racism.

Your holy worship dismantles the foul spirit of racism into jumbled pieces that are not able to reassemble into its orginal design to attack you again in the same manner.

The power of your holy worship transforms you into a conqueror of the obnoxious spirit of racism and its willing and racist human hosts.

Romans 8:35-39; John 4:23-24; Ephesians 6:16-18; Acts 16:25-26

127

Your true worship of God removes the "in" from "injustice" and releases true justice to you, the worshipper.

God's Holy written Word (the Bible) and His Living Word (Jesus Christ) are tangible in your life. Just believe!

God's Word, the Sword of the Spirit, is your ultimate, victorious weapon over racism! Use it! Apply it against the vile spirit of racism.

God's Holy Word is loaded in you; so you are God's battleaxe against the odious spirit of racism.

John 4:23-24; Ephesians 6:16-18; Acts 16:25-26; Jeremiah 51:20-23

128

Your true worship causes the demons of racism to take to their heels and flee for the gates of Hades where they belong.

Your true worship in the secret place of the Most High God takes you under His holy shadow.

The power of the impenetrable Shield of Faith, your faith in God through Jesus Christ, empowers you to overcome the injustice of racism.

Jesus Christ has freed you from the illegitimate and evil domination of the foul spirit of racism.

Jesus Christ has made you free from the yoke of the burden of racism.

You have the victory of Jesus Christ over racism!

Acts 16:25-26; Isaiah 10:27; John 4:23-24; James 4:7

129

You are not a "slave" to racism, but to God and His righteousness

through Christ Jesus.

Christ has set you free from the sin of racism.

So, you have become subject only to God, and through Jesus Christ you have gained His fruit of holiness, one that racism can never defile in you.

You are a child of God in Jesus Christ and cannot allow racism to cause you to live with a defeated soul.

Jesus Christ has set and made you free from the captivity of the vile spirit of racism—from its evil strangehold.

Romans 6:20-23; John 8:32,36; Isaiah 61:1-3; John 16:33

130

You are a child of God in Jesus Christ who will partake of the promises of God, Who has already declared for you both spiritual and material success.

God's truth has set you free from captivity, and unshackled your mind from mental slavery and oppression of racism.

God has flooded you with His spiritual knowledge and wisdom. Receive it!

Through Jesus Christ you have daily victory over racism.

John 8:32,36; Isaiah 61:1-4; Ephesians 1:18-23; Galatians 5:1

131

he Word of God makes it clear that it was never His design for

mankind to be under the bondage of physical or mental slavery, or racism.

It has never been God's design for you or any child of His to allow racism to cause you to live with a defeated mind.

Despite the racism you may face daily, God's design for you is to live victoriously.

God has heard your cry for help; He has heard and received your prayers against the wickedness and oppression of racism—and He will deliver you everytime you cry out to Him for help!

Romans 6:20-23,8:15; 1 John 5:4; 2 Timothy 1:7; Jeremiah 29:11, 33:3; Exodus 3:7; Galatians 4:6; Psalms 91:14-15

132

esus Christ shed His Blood on the cross of Calvary for the salvation of mankind and lifted the curse from us. He justified and reconciled us to God.

Therefore, racism lacks the power to place any curse or condemnation on you.

Racism cannot label you unclean when God says you are clean through Jesus Christ.

Through Jesus Christ, God has freed you from the evil grip of the vile spirit of racism and its racist human hosts.

Romans 6:18; 6:22-23; Revelation 1:5b; 1 Corinthians 6:11; 2 Corinthians 5:18-19; Colossians 1:20; Romans 8:1

133

*O*nly God has real power and authority over your career and life.

Only God and you can set the limits of your career's and life's success.

It is God, and not humans, Who gives us the power to get wealth.

Human power is an illusion without God's power backing it.

Put your faith, trust and confidence only in God through Jesus Christ.

Deuteronomy 8:18; 28:1-14; Psalms 75:6-7; Jeremiah 29:11; Psalms 118:8-9

134

Any negative thought of your person or life is not of God but of the devil

and must be held captive and demolished by the Holy Word and promises of God.

If God says you can, then you can! If you receive and keep His Holy Word in your heart and mind, then you can!

Reject the rejection of racism and racists!

Reject the lies of racism and racists!

Rebuke, renounce and veto racism by the awesome power of God's Holy Word and His Holy Spirit in you!

2 Corinthians 10:3-6; Joshua 1:7-9

135

If you believe in your heart and profess with your mouth that you are

saved through Jesus Christ, then you are saved.

Having now been saved, Jesus Christ is in you and you have become a new creation and old things have passed away.

Do not allow the foul spirit of racism to condemn you in your heart and mind!

Do not receive the lies and condemnation of racism!

Always reject racism and the negative words of racists!

Romans 8:1, 10:9; 2 Corinthians 5:17; Galatians 2:20

136

*G*od designed you to have a godly self-image.

God is the greatest builder and rebuilder of your true self-image.

God is the refiner and purifier of your true self-image.

Don't allow the foul spirit of racism or the negative words and actions of racists to distort in your heart and mind your view of who you are.

You are a beautiful child of the Most High God created in the excellent Image of God and renewed in Jesus Christ.

Genesis 1:26-27; Malachi 3:2-3; Jeremiah 18:1-6

137

*Y*our old self has been crucified with Christ, Who now lives in you, and you live by faith in Christ, Who loves you and Who gave Himself for you. This is the foundation of your true spiritual image that is solidly built in Jesus Christ.

By immersing yourself in the Holy Word of God, which is all knowing and truth, you will develop a positive self-esteem that the world cannot tamper with.

If you read, know, receive and believe in your heart God and His Holy Word, you immerse your heart and mind in the Word and racism will lose its "giant" status in your mind and will become a powerless peon against your life.

Romans 12:2; Galatians 2:20; 2 Corinthians 5:17; 1 Samuel 17:41-57

138

*Y*ou are born again with authentic spiritual nature of Jesus Christ

in you—and your renewed mind in Him.

To have a godly self-image means to be at peace with who and what you are, to have a sense of purpose, direction and confidence that you can and will succeed in life through Jesus Christ.

When you enter into God's rest through the knowledge of His Holy Word, you will be at peace with who you are because you know your true identity and nature in Jesus Christ.

Romans 12:2; Jeremiah 29:11; Isaiah 26:3-4; Philippians 3:7-11; 1 Corinthians 2:16

139

*G*od can burn off you the impurities of the effects of racism that have

settled in your soul and that have become encrusted in your heart and mind.

Your Christ-rooted self-esteem arises from your authentic spiritual knowledge
about who and what you are.

Your Christ-rooted self-regard, self-respect, self-acceptance, self-confidence and
self-esteem enable you to tackle any challenges and obstacles you may encounter.

Your Christ-rooted self-regard, self-respect, self-acceptance, self-confidence and
self-esteem will resist any negative impact of racism on your life.

Malachi 3:2-3; Romans 8:37; Philippians 4:13; Romans 8:37

140

You have to learn to say no to negative thoughts that attack your self-regard, self-respect, self-acceptance and self-esteem, and replace such bad thoughts with whatever is good, lovely, admirable, true, beautiful and positive.

True self-regard, self-respect, self-acceptance, self-confidence and self-esteem arises from authentic spiritual knowledge, understanding and wisdom of God.

Believe, read and know God's Holy Word and meditate on it daily; let it shape your mindset and mold your -regard, self-respect, self-acceptance, self-confidence and self-esteem.

Philippians 4:8-9; Ephesians 1:15-23, 4:20-23; Romans 12:2

141

*S*elf-acceptance is how comfortable you are with what and who you are.

Godly self-acceptance does not negate self-improvement, but lays the foundation of peace about who you are in Jesus Christ and the knowledge of the foundation of your true self-image in God.

Being rooted in Jesus Christ is the foundation for true self-acceptance.

Ephesians 2:10; Jeremiah 31:3; Jeremiah 1:4-7; Isaiah 43:7; Psalms 139:13-14; Jeremiah 31:3

142

*J*esus Christ is within you and has set the foundation for your intrinsic value and worth that is not based on external opinions or situations.

Your Christ-rooted confidence in the mental abilities and capabilities God has given to you fuels your self-efficacy and self-efficency.

God's grace through Jesus Christ is more than sufficient for you to overcome racism.

You are more than a conqueror through Jesus Christ over the vile spirit of racism.

1 Corinthians 8:2-3; Romans 12:3; Hebrews 10:35; Romans 8:37; Philippians 4:13; Jeremiah 31:3

143

Your self-respect is tied to your self-worth; it is your belief that you have inherent value of self-worth in Jesus Christ.

If you feel worthy of yourself, you acknowledge that you deserve the respect and love of others, but you affirm the truth that your self-worth does not depend on validation by others but on God's only truth about what and who you truly are.

God has justified and validated you through Jesus Christ—and you are sanctified through Him.

You are a child of God—His heir and co-heir with Jesus Christ.

Genesis 1:26-27; Ephesians 2:19; Colossians 1:12; Ephesians 2:11-13; Revelation 3:12; Philippians 1:27; Jeremiah 31:3; Romans 3:24-25; 4:5; 5:1,18; Romans 8:15-17; 1 Corinthians 1:30

144

*T*he greatest strategy that you can apply against any form of evil, including racism, is to fortify the truth of God's Holy Word within you.

You must sustain your spiritual fight against racism with the Holy Word of God firmly rooted within you.

God's Holy Word is the absolute truth about who you are in Jesus Christ— and racism cannot change this!

Hebrews 4:12-13; 2 Timothy 3:16; Ephesians 6:10-18; 2 Timothy 2:15; 1 John 4:4

145

esus Christ has defeated all evil for you, including racism, and He has

overcome the world on your behalf; by faith, stand in Him.

Build your faith on the Holy Word—on the Eternal Rock of Ages—Jesus Christ.

Your body is a temple of God in which His Holy Spirit dwells; therefore, racism has no authority or legal access to your spirit and your heart and mind are empowered to overcome it.

Jesus Christ has given you the authority to trample upon evil such as racism; and only you can allow the vile spirit of racism to walk over you.

Exercise the authority of Jesus Christ over the serpent and scorpion spirit of spirit of racism.

1 Corinthians 6:19-20; John 16:33; Luke 10:18-19; Matthew 7:24-27

146

*T*hrough Christ Jesus, God has freed you from the kingdom of dark-

ness; therefore, racism has no power or rule over you, and you cannot give racism any unauthorized access to your spirit, body and soul!

Through Jesus Christ, God has equipped your spirit to rule over racism and not for racism to rule over you.

Exercise the authority and power of Jesus Christ in you to rule over the foul spirit of racism and its wicked, oppressive and unjust actions orchestrated through its willing human hosts.

Colossians 1:13-14; 1 Corinthians 6:11; Luke 10:17-19; 1 Corinthians 6:19-20

147

*R*acism is from the kingdom of darknes; therefore, reject all lies

from and through racism and the foul spirit behind it.

Racism cannot reverse God's absolute truth about who you are in Christ Jesus.

Racism cannot change God's love and promises for your life.

Racism is a lie of the devil who is the father of all lies.

When racism rejects you, always reject the rejection of racism!

1 Thessalonians 5:22; John 8:44; Ephesians 5:8; 2 Corinthians 5:17; 2 Corinthians 1: 21-22; John 8:44; Jeremiah 29:11; Romans 8:35-39

148

*J*esus Christ has freed you from the oppression of racism, and now you

have liberty in Him.

You are free from the condemnation of racism, and because Christ has accepted you, no one is qualified to reject you.

To be rejected by racists is a wicked lie of the devil from the pit of hell.

You are the child of the Most High God, accepted into His Kingdom and loaded with His Kingdom power through Jesus Christ.

You are a citizen of the glorious Kingdom of God.

The gates of Hades will never prevail against your life through racism and or any other form of evil.

Romans 8:1; Galatians 5:1; Colossians 1:13-14, John 8:32,36; Matthew 16:18-19; Ephesians 2:19

149

*T*hrough Christ Jesus, you have defensive and offensive spiritual weap-

ons to resist the devil's tactics and strategies against you in any form—to resist racism and the wicked and evil activities of racists.

You have been selected, appointed and anointed to be fruitful in Jesus Christ, and racism lacks the power to render you unfruitful.

Despite racism you need to trust God and His Holy Word—believing that through Jesus Christ you are blessed and so are your children and your future generations to come.

Ephesians 6:10-18; 2 Corinthians 10:3-6; Luke 10:17-19; Genesis 1:26-27; Genesis 1:28; Genesis 9:7

150

*W*ith you and within you is God's Mantle of Victory over racism

God's Holy Word is like a matchstick that lights a blazing and consuming fire upon the foul spirit of racism.

You have power thoughts against the foul spirit of racism! Use them!

You have the awesome power of God in you through Jesus Christ over every principality, powers of darkness and spiritual wickedness in high places; so you are empowered through Christ to claim victory over racism.

You are indeed victorious over the vile spirit of racism and its human hosts.

Despite racism, receive God's truth that there is only one true race — the human race!

Hebrews 12:28-29; 1 John 4:4; 1 John 5:4; Philippians 4:7-9

∞∞∞∞∞∞∞∞∞ ♦ ♦ ♦ ♦ ♦ ∞∞∞∞∞∞∞∞∞

$\mathcal{G}$od's Holy Word for Power Thoughts

Using your preferred Holy Bible version, find, read and meditate on the referenced Scripture below, as God's Holy Spirit leads you, and let Him minister to you with His power of revelation knowledge. Let the precious Blood of our Lord and Savior Jesus Christ cleanse your heart and mind of the toxic deposits from your experiences with racism, and unshackle you from the stranglehold of the odious spirit of racism forever.

Allow God's Holy Word to begin the process of renewing your mind, and let it transform into your minute-by-minute power thoughts. Let God's power thoughts become the predominant thoughts that direct your heart, mind, thoughts, emotions, will and resolve, against the foul spirit of racism.

∞∞∞∞∞∞∞∞∞ ♦ ♦ ♦ ♦ ♦ ∞∞∞∞∞∞∞∞∞

∞∞∞∞∞∞∞∞∞∞ ◆ ◆ ◆ ◆ ◆ ∞∞∞∞∞∞∞∞∞∞

The Power of Our Salvation through Jesus Christ

(Receive God's Plan of Salvation)

- John 3:16,17,36
- Romans 10:9-10
- John 1:12
- Romans 3:22-24
- Romans 5:12
- Romans 5:8 / Romans 6:23
- Titus 3:5-6
- Psalms 106:8
- 1 John 4:14 / I John 5:11-13
- 2 Timothy 1:8b-9
- Luke 1:46b-47
- Luke 19:10
1 Corinthians 15:1-4
- 2 Corinthians 5:17
- Romans 10:8-10
- Ephesians 2:4-5,8-9
- Matthew 10:32
- John 6:47
- Revelation 3:20

∞∞∞∞∞∞∞∞∞∞ ◆ ◆ ◆ ◆ ◆ ∞∞∞∞∞∞∞∞∞∞

∞∞∞∞∞∞∞∞∞ ♦ ♦ ♦ ♦ ♦ ∞∞∞∞∞∞∞∞∞

The Power of the Lordship of Jesus Christ Over Racism

- Acts 2:25-28, 34-35
- Mark 12:30
- Isaiah 50:7
- Philippians 2:9-11
- Romans 10:9-10
- Luke 6:46
- Luke 10:18-19
- Psalms 27:4-6
- Psalms 86:5
- Psalms 68:19
- Psalms 73:28
- Psalms 110:1-2
- Matthew 28:18
- Romans 6:13-16
- Romans 12:1-2
- 1 Corinthians 6:19-20
- 1 Corinthians 15:28
- Romans 8:1, 14:8
- Hebrews 2:8

∞∞∞∞∞∞∞∞∞ ♦ ♦ ♦ ♦ ♦ ∞∞∞∞∞∞∞∞∞

∞∞∞∞∞∞∞∞∞∞ ♦ ♦ ♦ ♦ ♦ ∞∞∞∞∞∞∞∞∞∞

The Power of God's Holy Love Over Racism

- Romans 8:38-39
- 1 Corinthians 13:13
- Psalms 42:8
- John 14:21
- Romans 5:8
- John 3:16
- 1 John 4:7-12
- 1 John 4:16,19
- John 15:9-13, 17
- Ephesians 3:17-19
- Proverbs 8:17
- Jeremiah 31:3
- Hosea 2:19
- Isaiah 54:10
- Psalms 27:4-6,10

∞∞∞∞∞∞∞∞∞∞ ♦ ♦ ♦ ♦ ♦ ∞∞∞∞∞∞∞∞∞∞

∞∞∞∞∞∞∞∞∞ ♦ ♦ ♦ ♦ ∞∞∞∞∞∞∞∞∞

The Power of God's Peace Over Racism

- Philippians 4:6-9
- John 14:27
- John 16:33
- John 20:19
- Psalms 4:8
- Psalms 29:11
- Psalms 46:10
- Colossians 3:15
- Romans 5:1
- Isaiah 12:2
- Isaiah 26:3,12
- Isaiah 54:10
- Ephesians 2:13-14
- Isaiah 9:6-7
- Romans 16:20
- Matthew 11:28-30

∞∞∞∞∞∞∞∞∞ ♦ ♦ ♦ ♦ ∞∞∞∞∞∞∞∞∞

∞∞∞∞∞∞∞∞∞ ♦ ♦ ♦ ♦ ♦ ∞∞∞∞∞∞∞∞∞

The Power of Forgiveness

- Mark 11:25
- Psalms 32:1-2
- Isaiah 1:18
- Jeremiah 33:8
- Ephesians 1:5-7
- Psalms 85:2
- 2 Corinthians 5:17
- Psalms 103:12
- 1 John 2:1
- 1 John 1:9
- Isaiah 43:18,25
- Hebrews 8:12
- Isaiah 55:7
- Proverbs 28:13
- Colossians 2:13
- Colossians 3:13
- 1 John 1:9
- Matthew 5:44
- 1 Peter 3:9-10

194

- Ephesians 4:31-32
- Philippians 3:13-14
- Matthew 6:14-15
- Matthew 18:21-22
- Luke 17:3-4
- Romans 12:21

∞∞∞∞∞∞∞∞∞∞ ♦ ♦ ♦ ♦ ♦ ∞∞∞∞∞∞∞∞∞∞

∞∞∞∞∞∞∞∞∞∞ ◆ ◆ ◆ ◆ ◆ ∞∞∞∞∞∞∞∞∞∞

𝔗he Power of the Righteousness of Jesus Christ

- 2 Corinthians 5:21
- 1 Corinthians 1:30
- Philippians 3:8-9
- Galatians 3:6-7
- Romans 3:22
- Romans 3:23-26
- Romans 4-5
- Romans 5:17
- Titus 3:4-5
- Romans 8:3-4
- Romans 9:30
- Romans 8:10
- Romans 8:29-30
- Isaiah 54:14-17
- Romans 10:10

∞∞∞∞∞∞∞∞∞∞ ◆ ◆ ◆ ◆ ◆ ∞∞∞∞∞∞∞∞∞∞

∞∞∞∞∞∞∞∞∞∞ ♦ ♦ ♦ ♦ ♦ ∞∞∞∞∞∞∞∞∞∞

*A*re You Seeking Deliverance from Racism?

- Romans 6:22, 8:2, 12:2
  - Ephesians 4:23-24
    - Isaiah 61:1
    - John 8:32,36
    - Isaiah 10:17
    - Psalms 35, 37
    - Isaiah 10:27
  - 2 Corinthians 3:17
  - Deuteronomy 8:3
    - Matthew 4:4
    - Isaiah 9:3-4
    - Luke 4:18-19
    - Mark 16:17
  - Revelation 12:11
  - 1 John 4:1-4
  - Psalms 35, 37, 91
- Psalms 142, 143, 144

∞∞∞∞∞∞∞∞∞∞ ♦ ♦ ♦ ♦ ♦ ∞∞∞∞∞∞∞∞∞∞

∞∞∞∞∞∞∞∞∞∞∞ ♦ ♦ ♦ ♦ ∞∞∞∞∞∞∞∞∞∞∞

The Power of Holy Relationship and Fellowship With

God Over Racism

- 1 John 1:3
- 1 Corinthians 1:9
- Revelation 3:20
- John 14:23
- Zechariah 2:10
- Matthew 18:20
- John 14:21,23
- John 15:4-5,7,15
- Philippians 2:1-2
- Psalms 34:1-3
- Psalms 37
- Psalms 91
- Psalms 119:63
- Ephesians 5:2,19,30
- 1 John 1:5-7
- James 2:23
- Jeremiah 15:15

∞∞∞∞∞∞∞∞∞∞∞ ♦ ♦ ♦ ♦ ∞∞∞∞∞∞∞∞∞∞∞

∞∞∞∞∞∞∞∞∞ ♦ ♦ ♦ ♦ ♦ ∞∞∞∞∞∞∞∞∞

When the Foul Spirit of Racism is Operating

Against You or Among You:

- Mark 16:17
- Luke 10:18-19
- Colossians 3:13
- Galatians 3:26-27
- Ephesians 2:19
- 1 John 3:1
- Galatians 4:6-7
- Romans 8:14
- Hebrews 4:12-13
- Romans 1:18-20
- Psalms 35
- Psalms 37
- Psalms 140
- Psalms 142
- Psalms 144

∞∞∞∞∞∞∞∞∞ ♦ ♦ ♦ ♦ ♦ ∞∞∞∞∞∞∞∞∞

∞∞∞∞∞∞∞∞∞ ◆ ◆ ◆ ◆ ◆ ∞∞∞∞∞∞∞∞∞

𝓝eeding God's Holy Protection Against Racism?

- Galatians 3:26-27
  - Psalms 3:3
  - Psalms 23
  - Psalms 35
  - Psalms 37
  - Psalms 91
  - Isaiah 43:2
- 2 Chronicles 16:9a
- Deuteronomy 1:30
- 2 Thessalonians 3:3
  - Exodus 23:22
  - 1 Samuel 2:9
  - Psalms 61:3
  - Zephaniah 3:17
  - 1 Peter 3:12-13
- Deuteronomy 33:27
  - Isaiah 59:19

∞∞∞∞∞∞∞∞∞ ◆ ◆ ◆ ◆ ◆ ∞∞∞∞∞∞∞∞∞

∞∞∞∞∞∞∞∞∞∞ ◆ ◆ ◆ ◆ ◆ ∞∞∞∞∞∞∞∞∞∞

Feeling Insecure or Intimidated By Racism?

- Hebrews 12:15
- 1 John 4:4
- 1 John 5:4
- Jude 24-25
- Psalms 18
- Psalms 23
- Psalms 25
- Psalms 91
- Psalms 35
- Psalms 37
- Joshua 1:7-9
- 2 Kings 6:8-20
- Isaiah 41:10
- Isaiah 40:26
- Philippians 1:6
- Romans 8:35-39
- John 10:27-30
- 2 Corinthians 1:22

∞∞∞∞∞∞∞∞∞∞∞∞ ◆ ◆ ◆ ◆ ◆ ∞∞∞∞∞∞∞∞∞∞∞∞

∞∞∞∞∞∞∞∞∞ ◆ ◆ ◆ ◆ ◆ ∞∞∞∞∞∞∞∞∞

When You are Discouraged By Racism

- Joshua 1:7-9
- 1 Peter 1:6-9
- Philippians 4:6-8
- Psalms 91:14-16
- Psalms 138:7
- John 14:1
- John 14:27
- 2 Corinthians 4:8-9
- Hebrews 10:35-36
- Philippians 1:6
- Galatians 6:9
- Psalms 31:24
- Hebrews 11:6
- Psalms 23
- Psalms 27:1-14
- Psalms 42
- Psalms 43

∞∞∞∞∞∞∞∞∞ ◆ ◆ ◆ ◆ ◆ ∞∞∞∞∞∞∞∞∞

∞∞∞∞∞∞∞∞∞∞∞ ◆ ◆ ◆ ◆ ◆ ∞∞∞∞∞∞∞∞∞∞∞

Are You Worried or Anxious About Racism?

- Psalms 23
- Psalms 27
- Psalms 35
- Psalms 37
- Psalms 54
- Psalms 55:22
- Psalms 56
- Psalms 91
- Psalms 97
- Psalms 142
- Psalms 143
- Psalms 14
- John 14:27
- Psalms 119:165
- Isaiah 26:3
- 1 Peter 5:6-7

∞∞∞∞∞∞∞∞∞∞∞ ◆ ◆ ◆ ◆ ◆ ∞∞∞∞∞∞∞∞∞∞∞

∞∞∞∞∞∞∞∞∞ ♦ ♦ ♦ ♦ ∞∞∞∞∞∞∞∞∞

When You Feel Alienated or Deserted By Racism

- Psalms 43:5
- Deuteronomy 31:6
- Psalms 46:1
- Romans 8:35-39
- 1 Peter 5:7
- Psalms 27:10
- Deuteronomy 4:31
- Psalms 147:3
- Deuteronomy 33:27
- John 14:1,18
- Isaiah 41:10
- 1 Samuel 12:22
- Matthew 28:20
- Psalms 9:10
- Psalms 94:14
- Psalms 27:10
- Matthew 28:20

- Isaiah 62:4
- 2 Corinthians 4:9
- 1 Peter 5:7
- 1 Samuel 12:22
- Psalms 37:25
- Isaiah 41:17
- Psalms 91:14-15
- Isaiah 49:15-16a

∞∞∞∞∞∞∞∞ ♦ ♦ ♦ ♦ ♦ ∞∞∞∞∞∞∞∞

∞∞∞∞∞∞∞∞∞ ♦ ♦ ♦ ♦ ♦ ∞∞∞∞∞∞∞∞∞

*A*re You Feeling Down Due to Racism?

- Psalms 23
- Psalms 34:17
- Isaiah 43:2
- Psalms 30:5
- Psalms 37:3
- Psalms 147:3
- Isaiah 61:3
- Isaiah 40:31
- Nehemiah 8:10
- 2 Corinthians 1:3-4
- Romans 8:35-39
- Philippians 4:8
- 1 Peter 4:12-13
- 1 Peter 5:6-7
- Luke 18:1
- Isaiah 41:10
- Isaiah 51:11
- Isaiah 12:2-3
- Jeremiah 31:14

∞∞∞∞∞∞∞∞∞ ♦ ♦ ♦ ♦ ♦ ∞∞∞∞∞∞∞∞∞

∞∞∞∞∞∞∞∞∞∞∞ ♦ ♦ ♦ ♦ ♦ ∞∞∞∞∞∞∞∞∞∞∞

*A*re You Ruled By the Foul Spirit of Racism?

(Feeling Condemned By the Foul Spirit of Racism?)

- Romans 8:1
- Hebrews 8:12
- Hebrews 10:22
- Psalms 32:1
- Psalms 32:5, 8
- Psalms 103:10,12
- Isaiah 43:25
- Isaiah 55:7
- 2 Chronicles 30:9
- Jeremiah 31:34
- John 3:17-18
- John 5:24
- John 8:10-11
- 1 John 1:9
- Galatians 5:1
- 2 Corinthians 5:17
- Revelation 12:10-11

∞∞∞∞∞∞∞∞∞∞∞∞ ♦ ♦ ♦ ♦ ♦ ∞∞∞∞∞∞∞∞∞∞∞

∞∞∞∞∞∞∞∞∞∞ ♦ ♦ ♦ ♦ ∞∞∞∞∞∞∞∞∞∞

Feeling Confused By Racism?

- Jeremiah 33:3
- 1 Corinthians 14:33a
- 2 Timothy 1:7
- James 3:16:18
- Isaiah 50:7
- 1 Peter 4:12-13
- James 1:5
- Proverbs 3:5-6
- Psalms 23
- Psalms 32:8
- Psalms 119:165
- Psalms 55:23
- Isaiah 43:2
- Isaiah 40:29
- Isaiah 30:21

∞∞∞∞∞∞∞∞∞∞ ♦ ♦ ♦ ♦ ∞∞∞∞∞∞∞∞∞∞

∞∞∞∞∞∞∞∞∞∞ ♦ ♦ ♦ ♦ ♦ ∞∞∞∞∞∞∞∞∞∞

*B*eing Tempted By a Racist Situation?

- Hebrews 4:14-16
- 2 Peter 2:9a
- 1 Corinthians 10:12-13
- Romans 6:14
- Psalms 119:11
- James 1:13-14
- 1 Peter 5:8-9
- Ephesians 6:10-18
- James 4:7
- 1 John 4:4
- James 1:2-3, 12
- Jude 24-25
- 1 Peter 1:6-7
- John 8:44
- Hebrews 4:15

∞∞∞∞∞∞∞∞∞∞ ♦ ♦ ♦ ♦ ♦ ∞∞∞∞∞∞∞∞∞∞

∞∞∞∞∞∞∞∞∞∞ ◆ ◆ ◆ ◆ ◆ ∞∞∞∞∞∞∞∞∞∞

Are You Experiecing Unrighteous Anger Due to Racism?

- James 1:19-20
- Ephesians 4:26
- Proverbs 15:1
- Matthew 6:14
- Proverbs 14:29
- Proverbs 16:32
- Ecclesiastes 7:9
- Romans 12:19
- Proverbs 25:21:22
- Hebrews 10:30
- Ephesians 4:31-32
- Matthew 5:22-24
- Proverbs 14:16-17
- Colossians 3:8
- Psalms 37:8

∞∞∞∞∞∞∞∞∞∞ ◆ ◆ ◆ ◆ ◆ ∞∞∞∞∞∞∞∞∞∞

∞∞∞∞∞∞∞∞∞∞ ♦ ♦ ♦ ♦ ♦ ∞∞∞∞∞∞∞∞∞∞

*A*re Your Experiences With Racism Causing You to

Have a Rebellious Spriit?

- Hebrews 13:17
- Proverbs 14:16-17
- I Samuel 15:22-23
- 1 Peter 1:13-14
- Isaiah 1:19-20
- 1 Peter 2:13-15
- Philippians 2:5-8
- Hebrews 5:8
- 1 Peter 1 5:5-6
- Ephesians 5:21
- Proverbs 12:21
- Romans 6:12-13
- Ephesians 4:17-18
- Ephesians 5:8
- James 4:7
- Ephesians 4:29

∞∞∞∞∞∞∞∞∞∞ ♦ ♦ ♦ ♦ ♦ ∞∞∞∞∞∞∞∞∞∞

∞∞∞∞∞∞∞∞∞∞ ◆ ◆ ◆ ◆ ◆ ∞∞∞∞∞∞∞∞∞∞

Feeling Rejected By Racism?

- Romans 8:1,37
- 1 Samuel 16:7b
- 1 Chronicles 28:9
- Psalms 1:1-3
- Psalms 34:18
- Psalms 37:5-7
- Psalms 84:11
- Psalms 115:12-13
- Matthew 5:10-12
- John 6:37
- Colossians 3:12-14
- 1 Peter 4:16
- Hebrews 4:16
- Proverbs 10:6,22,24
- Acts 10:34-35
- 1 Samuel 16:7
- John 7:24

∞∞∞∞∞∞∞∞∞∞ ◆ ◆ ◆ ◆ ◆ ∞∞∞∞∞∞∞∞∞∞

∞∞∞∞∞∞∞∞ ◆ ◆ ◆ ◆ ◆ ∞∞∞∞∞∞∞∞

Is Racism Making You Afraid?

- 2 Timothy 1:7
- Romans 8:15-16
- 1 John 4:18
- Psalms 91:1-2
- Isaiah 40:31
- Psalms 91:4-7
- Hebrews 13:6,8
- Psalms 91:10-11,14
- Proverbs 3:25-26
- Isaiah 54:14
- Psalms 56:11
- Psalms 23:4-5
- Romans 8:29, 31, 35-39
- Psalms 31:24
- John14:27
- Psalms 27:1,3
- Psalms 5:12
- Psalms 30:7-8

∞∞∞∞∞∞∞∞ ◆ ◆ ◆ ◆ ◆ ∞∞∞∞∞∞∞∞

∞∞∞∞∞∞∞∞∞∞ ♦ ♦ ♦ ♦ ♦ ∞∞∞∞∞∞∞∞∞∞

When Racism Makes You Doubt Yourself

- Philippians 4:13
- Romans 8:37
- Isaiah 41:10
- 1 Peter 2:6
- Isaiah 26:3-4
- Isaiah 43:2
- Isaiah 50:7
- Psalms 55:22-23
- Philippians 4:6-8
- Psalms 4:8
- Psalms 29:11
- Psalms 46:10
- Psalms 118:8
- Psalms 106:3
- Psalms 147:3
- 2 Corinthians 1:3-4
- Romans 8:38-39

∞∞∞∞∞∞∞∞∞∞ ♦ ♦ ♦ ♦ ♦ ∞∞∞∞∞∞∞∞∞∞

∞∞∞∞∞∞∞∞∞ ◆ ◆ ◆ ◆ ◆ ∞∞∞∞∞∞∞∞∞

*I*s Racism Causing You to Be Too Stressed To Be

Blessed?

- John 16:33
- Psalms 27:14
- Lamentations 3:25-26
- Romans 8:25-26
- Romans 12:1,12
- Hebrews 10:35-38
- Philippians 4:7-9
- Ecclesiates 7:8-9
- Galatians 5:22-23
- Psalms 34:1-10,13-22
- Psalms 35:1-3
- Psalms 37:7-8,16
- Psalms 40:1
- Psalms 42:1-11
- Romans 5:3-5
- James 1:2-4
- James 5:7-8

∞∞∞∞∞∞∞∞∞ ◆ ◆ ◆ ◆ ◆ ∞∞∞∞∞∞∞∞∞

∞∞∞∞∞∞∞∞∞∞ ♦ ♦ ♦ ♦ ∞∞∞∞∞∞∞∞∞∞

$\mathcal{I}$s Racism Causing You to Be Unhappy?

- John 16:33
- Isaiah 26:3-4
- John 14:27
- Philippians 4:6-9
- Romans 5:1-2
- Isaiah 25:8-9
- Isaiah 55:8-9,12
- Psalms 34:1-10, 13-22
- Psalms 35:1-3
- Psalms 37: 17:19, 39-40
- Psalms 42:1-11
- Romans 8:7-9
- Psalms 119:165-169
- Isaiah 57:19-21
- 2 Corinthians 4:6,8-9
- Romans 15:13

∞∞∞∞∞∞∞∞∞∞ ♦ ♦ ♦ ♦ ∞∞∞∞∞∞∞∞∞∞

∞∞∞∞∞∞∞∞∞∞ ♦ ♦ ♦ ♦ ♦ ∞∞∞∞∞∞∞∞∞∞

Is Racsim Causing You to Be Spiritually Complacent?

- Proverbs 3:3-6
- Psalms 84:11
- Revelation 3:2,15-16,19
- Revelation 2:4-5,7
- Hosea 14:2,4,9
- Deuteronomy 4:2,6,9
- Romans 12:2
- 1 John 1:9-10
- Deuteronomy 8:5-6,11,19
- Psalms 44:20-21
- Hebrews 3:12-13
- Hebrews 5:11-12
- 2 Peter 2:20-21
- Jeremiah 6:16
- Luke 9:62

∞∞∞∞∞∞∞∞∞∞ ♦ ♦ ♦ ♦ ♦ ∞∞∞∞∞∞∞∞∞∞

∞∞∞∞∞∞∞∞∞∞ ♦ ♦ ♦ ♦ ∞∞∞∞∞∞∞∞∞∞

𝒲hen Racism Makes You Doubt God's Word and

Power

- Mark 11:22-25
- Isaiah 46:10-11b
- 1 Thessalonians 5:23-24
- 2 Peter 3:9
- Psalms 18:30-32,36
- 1 Peter 4:12-14
- Romans 10:17
- Isaiah 55:3,6,10-11
- Isaiah 54:10
- 1 Peter 1:23-25
- Matthew 24:35
- Psalms 119:89
- Isaiah 40:8
- Matthew 5:18
- 1 Kings 8:56
- Jude 24-25

- Proverbs 4:20-22
- Romans 8:28,31
- Deuteronomy 33:3,27
- Psalms 40:2-3
- Psalms 46:1
- Psalms 27, 35, 37, 91
- Proverbs 18:10
- 2 Thessalonians 3:3

∞∞∞∞∞∞∞∞∞∞ ♦ ♦ ♦ ♦ ♦ ∞∞∞∞∞∞∞∞∞∞

∞∞∞∞∞∞∞∞∞ ♦ ♦ ♦ ♦ ∞∞∞∞∞∞∞∞∞

When Racism Attempts to Diminish Your Significance in Your Mind and Before Others?

- Philippians 4:13
- Hebrews 13:6
- Psalms 27:1-3
- Hebrews 10:35-36
- Philippians 1:6
- Ephesians 3:18-19
- Ephesians 4:22-23
- Romans 8:26-27
- Isaiah 40:31
- 1 John5:14-15
- Zechariah 4:6
- Isaiah 43:2
- Proverbs 3:25-26
- Ephesians 3:12
- 1 John 3:21
- John 14:12
- Deuteronomy 8:18
- Deuteronomy 28:1-14

∞∞∞∞∞∞∞∞∞ ♦ ♦ ♦ ♦ ∞∞∞∞∞∞∞∞∞

∞∞∞∞∞∞∞∞∞ ♦ ♦ ♦ ♦ ♦ ∞∞∞∞∞∞∞∞∞

*W*hen Racism Stresses Your Life:

- Psalms 23
- Psalms 35
- Psalms 37
- Psalms 91
- John 14:1
- Romans 8:28
- Nahum 1:7
- 2 Corinthians 4:8-9
- Psalms 138:7
- Psalms 68
- Isaiah 42:16
- Isaiah 51:11
- Psalms 31
- Psalms 121:1-2
- Hebrews 4:15-16
- 1 Peter 5:7
- Matthew 6:34
- 2 Corinthians 1:34
- Philippians 4:6-7
- Matthew 11:28-30

∞∞∞∞∞∞∞∞∞ ♦ ♦ ♦ ♦ ♦ ∞∞∞∞∞∞∞∞∞

∞∞∞∞∞∞∞∞ ♦ ♦ ♦ ♦ ∞∞∞∞∞∞∞∞

*A*re You Interceeding for a Victim of Racial Hate?

Are You Praying for a Family that Lost a Loved One to a Hate Crime?

- Psalms 23:4
- Psalms 25:1-5,9-10, 16-22
- Psalms 27:1-5
- Psalms 35, 37, 91, 109
- Psalms 93:3-5
- 1 Corinthians 15:55-58
- 1 Peter 5:7
- Hebrews 4:14-16
- Isaiah 41:10
- 2 Corinthians 5:8-10
- Isaiah 51:11,12-16
- Isaiah 52:1-6,9-15
- Psalms 119:41-50
- Revelation 21:4
- Isaiah 61:1-3
- 2 Corinthians 1:3-5
- Matthew 5:4
- 2 Thessalonians 2:16-17

222

- Isaiah 43:2-3a
- Isaiah 49:13b
- 1 Thessalonians 4:13-14

∞∞∞∞∞∞∞∞∞∞ ◆ ◆ ◆ ◆ ∞∞∞∞∞∞∞∞∞∞

∞∞∞∞∞∞∞∞∞ ♦ ♦ ♦ ♦ ∞∞∞∞∞∞∞∞∞

When God Seems to Be Silent About Racism

- Isaiah 55:8-9
- Jeremiah 33:3
- Romans 8:31
- Romans 8:35-39
- 1 Corinthians 10:13
- Psalms 27:1-5,7-14
- Psalms 32:7
- Psalms 34:1-7,19
- Psalms 42:1-11
- Psalms 68:1
- Psalms 72:1-6
- Psalms 93:3-5
- Psalms 108:12-13
- 1 Peter 4:12-13
- Isaiah 41:10
- Romans 8:28
- Hosea 6:1-3
- Psalms 18:30
- Hebrews 10:23
- Hebrews 11:1-6

- Jeremiah 32:40
- Psalms 138:8
- Psalms 36:11

∞∞∞∞∞∞∞∞∞ ♦ ♦ ♦ ♦ ∞∞∞∞∞∞∞∞∞

∞∞∞∞∞∞∞∞ ◆ ◆ ◆ ◆ ∞∞∞∞∞∞∞∞

When Racism Blocks Your Path

- Mark 11:23-25
- Mark 13:31
- Psalms 27:14
- Psalms 33:8-9, 20
- Psalms 37:34
- Psalms 62:5
- Psalms 119:11-12, 105
- Psalms 130:5
- Habakkuk 2:3
- Hebrews 4:12-13
- Hebrews 10:23
- Ephesians 5:15
- Isaiah 10:27
- Isaiah 40:31
- Isaiah 54:15,17
- Isaiah 55:11
- Isaiah 61:1-3
- Proverbs 30:5

- Acts 20:32
- Romans 8:15-17
- Colossians 3:23-24
- 2 Corinthians 1:20-21

∞∞∞∞∞∞∞∞∞ ♦ ♦ ♦ ♦ ♦ ∞∞∞∞∞∞∞∞∞

∞∞∞∞∞∞∞∞∞∞ ◆ ◆ ◆ ◆ ∞∞∞∞∞∞∞∞∞∞

When Racism Makes You Weary

- Matthew 11:28
- Ephesians 3:16-17
Ephesians 6:10, 13-14
Psalms 1:1-3
- Psalms 18:1-3
Psalms 23:1-3
Psalms 25:1-5
- Psalms 27:1-2
Psalms 34:1-10
Psalms 35:1-10
- Psalms 119:28
- Proverbs 8:14
- Isaiah 30:15
- Isaiah 40:29-31
- Isaiah 41:10
- Philippians 4:13
- Nehemiah 8:10
- Colossians 1:11-12
- Daniel 10:17-19

∞∞∞∞∞∞∞∞∞∞ ◆ ◆ ◆ ◆ ∞∞∞∞∞∞∞∞∞∞

∞∞∞∞∞∞∞∞∞ ◆ ◆ ◆ ◆ ◆ ∞∞∞∞∞∞∞∞∞∞

The Power of Your Faith Against Racism

- Hebrews 11:1
- Hebrewa 11:3
- Romans 10:17
- Romans 12:3
- Hebrews 12:1-2
- Matthew 17:20
- Mark 11:22-24
- Mark 9:23-24
- Romans 1:17
- 2 Corinthians 5:7
- Hebrews 11:6
- 1 Peter 1:7-9
- 1 John 5:3-5
- Matthew 9:20-22
- Matthew 9:28-29
- James 5:14-15

∞∞∞∞∞∞∞∞∞ ◆ ◆ ◆ ◆ ◆ ∞∞∞∞∞∞∞∞∞∞

∞∞∞∞∞∞∞∞∞ ◆ ◆ ◆ ◆ ◆ ∞∞∞∞∞∞∞∞∞

The Power of Your Praise Over Racism

- Acts 16:25
- Psalms 96:4-8
- Psalms 92:1-2, 4-5
- Psalms 71:5-8
- Psalms 63:3-5
- Psalms 50:23
- Psalms 48:1
- Psalms 47:1-2,6-7
- Ephesians 5:18-20
- Psalms 107:8
- Psalms 107:8
- Psalms 34:1-3
- Isaiah 43:21
- I Peter 2:9
- Hebrews 13:14-15
- Psalms 147:1
- 2 Samuel 22:4

∞∞∞∞∞∞∞∞∞ ◆ ◆ ◆ ◆ ◆ ∞∞∞∞∞∞∞∞∞

∞∞∞∞∞∞∞∞∞ ♦ ♦ ♦ ♦ ♦ ∞∞∞∞∞∞∞∞∞

𝒯he Power of Thanksgiving to God Over Racism

- Hebrews 12:28-29
- Psalms 28:7
- Psalms 34:1
- Psalms 69:30
- Psalms 75:1
- Psalms 95:1-6
- Psalms 100:4
- Psalms 100:1-5
- Psalms 107:1,29-32
- Psalms136:1-26
- Colossians 2:6-7
- 1 Chronicles 16:8,34
- Jonah 2:9
- Ephesians 5:3-4
- Colossians 3:15
- 1 Timothy 4:4-5
- 1 Thessalonians 5:18
- Philippians 4:6
- Luke 17:15-19
- 1 Thessalonians 5:18
- Colossians 2:6-7
- Isaiah 12:1-6

∞∞∞∞∞∞∞∞∞ ♦ ♦ ♦ ♦ ♦ ∞∞∞∞∞∞∞∞∞

∞∞∞∞∞∞∞∞∞∞ ♦ ♦ ♦ ♦ ♦ ∞∞∞∞∞∞∞∞∞∞

The Power of Your Holy Worship Over Racism

- Psalms 100:4
- Romans 12:1-2
- Exodus 33:9-10
- Hebrews 5:7
- Exodus 15:20-21
- Galatians 2:20
- Psalms 8:1
- Psalms 29:2
- Psalms 95:6
- Psalms 99:5
- John 4:21-24
- Deuteronomy 12:5-7
- Philippians 2:9-11
- James 4:8
- Revelation 5:9
- Revelation 4:11
- Psalms 59:16
- Psalms 63:3-4
- Psalms 66:4
- Psalms 150

∞∞∞∞∞∞∞∞∞∞ ♦ ♦ ♦ ♦ ♦ ∞∞∞∞∞∞∞∞∞∞

∞∞∞∞∞∞∞∞ ◆ ◆ ◆ ◆ ◆ ∞∞∞∞∞∞∞∞

𝔗he Power of Knowing The Holy Spirit Over Racism

- 1 Corinthians 6:19
- Romans 5:5
- John 14:16-20
- John 16:7-9, 14
- Matthew 3:11
- John 7:38-39
- Acts 19:1-6
- Galatians 5:16-17
- Acts 1:4-5,7-8
- Acts 3:28
- Acts 4:31
- Ephesians 5:18-20
- Acts 8:14-17
- Acts 10:44-47

∞∞∞∞∞∞∞∞ ◆ ◆ ◆ ◆ ◆ ∞∞∞∞∞∞∞∞

∞∞∞∞∞∞∞∞∞∞ ♦ ♦ ♦ ♦ ∞∞∞∞∞∞∞∞∞∞

The Power of Trusting God's Faithfulness Over Racism

- Psalms 24, 25, 26, 27
- Psalms 119:64-65
- 1 Thessalonians 5:23-24
- Isaiah 54:9-10
- Genesis 9:16-17
- Genesis 28:15
- 1 Corinthians 1:9
- 1 Corinthians 10:13
- 2 Timothy 2:13,19
- Deuteronomy 7:8-9
- Joshua 23:14
- 1 Kings 8:56-58
- Psalms 36:5
- Psalms 89:1-2,19,34
- - Psalms 121:3,7-8
- 2 Peter 3:9

∞∞∞∞∞∞∞∞∞∞ ♦ ♦ ♦ ♦ ∞∞∞∞∞∞∞∞∞∞

∞∞∞∞∞∞∞∞∞ ♦ ♦ ♦ ♦ ∞∞∞∞∞∞∞∞∞

𝒯he Power of Spiritual Warfare Over Racism

- Ephesians 6:10-18
- 2 Timothy 2:3-4
- Romans 16:20
- 2 Thessalonians 1:6-7
- Deuteronomy 18:10-14
- 1 Thessalonians 5:8
- Isaiah 53:11-12
- 2 Corinthians 10:34
- 2 Timothy 4:18
- 1 Peter 5:8
- Hebrews 2:14-15
- James 4:7
- Luke 10:18-19
- Colossians 1:13-14
- Revelation 12:10-11
- Mark 4:39
- Mark 11:23
- Psalms 35, 37, 91

∞∞∞∞∞∞∞∞∞ ♦ ♦ ♦ ♦ ∞∞∞∞∞∞∞∞∞

∞∞∞∞∞∞∞∞∞∞ ◆ ◆ ◆ ◆ ◆ ∞∞∞∞∞∞∞∞∞∞

Focusing on God's Holy Will for Your Life

(Despite the Racism You Face)

- Jeremiah 29:11
- Proverbs 16:3
- 3 John 2
- Deuteronomy 8:18
- Deuteronomy 28:1-14
- James 1:5-6
- Psalms 32:8
- Psalms 119:105-106
- Proverbs 6:20,22-23
- Joshua 1:8-9
- Isaiah 30:21
- Psalms 48:14
- 1 Thessalonians 4:3-4,6
- 1 Thessalonians 5:16-18
- Colossians 1:3,9-10
- Colossians 3:15-17
- Psalms 143:10

236

- 1 Timothy 2:1,3-4
- Psalms 37:23:24
- Psalms 31:3,5
- Hebrews 11:6
- Proverbs 3:1,5-6,11-12
- Isaiah 48:17
- Isaiah 58:11
- John 16:13-14
- Romans 8:14
- Romans 12:2
- Ephesians 5:17

∞∞∞∞∞∞∞∞ ♦ ♦ ♦ ♦ ∞∞∞∞∞∞∞∞

∞∞∞∞∞∞∞∞∞∞ ♦ ♦ ♦ ♦ ∞∞∞∞∞∞∞∞∞∞

*R*emaining Steadfast in Prayer

(Even as You Experience Racism)

- Psalms 91:14-16
- Isaiah 65:24
- Jeremiah 33:2-3
- Matthew 7:7-8
- Mattew 21:22
- Matthew 18:19-20
- Mark 11:24-25
- John 14:13-14
- John 15:7
- Matthew 6:6
- John 16:23
- Hebrews 4:16
- Psalms 37:4-5
- Psalms 145:18-20
- Proverbs 15:29
- 1 John 3:22-24
- 1 Thessalonians 5:17

∞∞∞∞∞∞∞∞∞∞ ♦ ♦ ♦ ♦ ∞∞∞∞∞∞∞∞∞∞

∞∞∞∞∞∞∞∞∞ ♦ ♦ ♦ ♦ ∞∞∞∞∞∞∞∞∞∞

The Power of Daily Spiritual Growth Over Racism

- Hebrews 11:1-3,32-34
  - 2 Peter 3:18
  - 1 Peter 2:2-3
  - 2 Timothy 2:15
  - 1 Timothy 4:15
  - Hebrews 6:1
  - Galatians 6:9
  - 2 Peter 1:5-8
- Ephesians 3:14-19
- Colossians 1:9-11
- Colossians 3:16
- 2 Corinthians 3:18
  - Psalms 1:1-3
  - Psalms 93:12
- Philippians 1:6,9-10
- Ephesians 4:14-16
- Matthew 5:14-16
  - Daniel 12:3
  - 1 John 5:3-5

- Galatians 5:22-23
- Romans 12:2
- Colossians 3:23-24
- 1 Peter 2:9-12
- Acts 17:30
- Romans 10:14

∞∞∞∞∞∞∞∞∞∞ ◆ ◆ ◆ ◆ ◆ ∞∞∞∞∞∞∞∞∞∞

General Notes

♣ ♣ ♣ ♣ ♣

Date:_____**Topic:**_____

_____

Date:_____**Topic:**_____

_____

Date:_____**Topic:**_____

_____

Date:_____**Topic:**_____

_____

Date:_____**Topic:**_____

_____

Date:_____**Topic:**_____

_____

Date:_____**Topic:**_____

_____

Date: _____ **Topic:** _____

_____

Date:_____**Topic:**_____

_____

Available:

'RAYS OF VICTORY' SERIES

This Book is:

150 POWER THOUGHTS FOR VICTORY OVER RACISM

Power of a Christ-rooted Mindset Over Racism

∞∞∞∞∞∞∞∞ ♦ ♦ ♦ ♦ ♦ ∞∞∞∞∞∞∞∞

Excerpts from "Nailing Racism to the Cross"

∞∞∞∞∞∞∞∞ ♦ ♦ ♦ ♦ ♦ ∞∞∞∞∞∞∞∞

Dr. Jacyee Aniagolu-Johnson

First Paperback Edition
ISBN 978-1-937-230-00-5

Also Available:

'RAYS OF VICTORY' SERIES

POWER THOUGHTS

Diary

FOR VICTORY OVER RACISM

Journal for Power Thoughts Against Racism
[With Excerpts from "Nailing Racism to the Cross"]

Dr. Jacyee Aniagolu-Johnson

First Paperback Edition:
ISBN: 978-1-937230-04-3

'RAYS OF VICTORY' SERIES

150 SIGN POSTS TO VICTORY OVER RACISM

(Volume 1)

Empowering Sign Posts for Victory Over Racism

∞∞∞∞∞∞∞∞∞∞ ♦ ♦ ♦ ♦ ♦ ∞∞∞∞∞∞∞∞∞∞

Excerpts from "Nailing Racism to the Cross"

∞∞∞∞∞∞∞∞∞∞ ♦ ♦ ♦ ♦ ♦ ∞∞∞∞∞∞∞∞∞∞

By
Dr. Jacyee Aniagolu-Johnson

First Paperback Edition
ISBN 978-1-937230-01-2

'RAYS OF VICTORY' SERIES

150 SIGN POSTS TO VICTORY OVER RACISM

(Volume 2)

Empowering Sign Posts for Victory Over Racism

∞∞∞∞∞∞∞∞∞∞ ♦ ♦ ♦ ♦ ♦ ∞∞∞∞∞∞∞∞∞∞

Excerpts from "Nailing Racism to the Cross"

∞∞∞∞∞∞∞∞∞∞ ♦ ♦ ♦ ♦ ♦ ∞∞∞∞∞∞∞∞∞∞

By
Dr. Jacyee Aniagolu-Johnson

First Paperback Edition
ISBN 978-1-937230-02-9

'RAYS OF VICTORY' SERIES

150 SIGN POSTS TO

VICTORY OVER

RACISM

(Volume 3)

Empowering Sign Posts for Victory Over Racism

∞∞∞∞∞∞∞∞ ♦ ♦ ♦ ♦ ♦ ∞∞∞∞∞∞∞∞

188B Excerpts from "Nailing Racism to the Cross"

∞∞∞∞∞∞∞∞ ♦ ♦ ♦ ♦ ♦ ∞∞∞∞∞∞∞∞

By
Dr. Jacyee Aniagolu-Johnson

First Paperback Edition
ISBN 978-1-937230-03-6

'RAYS OF VICTORY' SERIES

WORKBOOK SERIES

FOOTPRINTS OF

VICTORY OVER

RACISM

In the Secret Place With God

(Volume 1)

Illuminating Daily Guideposts for God's Rays of Victory Over Racism

By
Dr. Jacyee Aniagolu-Johnson

First Paperback Edition
ISBN 978-0-9789669-5-9

'RAYS OF VICTORY' SERIES

WORKBOOK SERIES

FOOTPRINTS OF

VICTORY OVER

RACISM

In the Secret Place With God

(Volume 2)

*Illuminating Daily Guideposts for God's Rays of
Victory Over Racism*

By
Dr. Jacyee Aniagolu-Johnson

First Paperback Edition
ISBN 978-0-9789669-6-6

'RAYS OF VICTORY' SERIES

ON THE HAMMOCK: WITH THE SWORD OF THE SPIRIT

FOR INDIVIDUAL VICTORY OVER RACISM

A Meditation Journal
[40 Days of Daily Meditation]
(Volume 1)

By
Dr. Jacyee Aniagolu-Johnson

First Paperback Edition
ISBN 978-0-9789669-8-0

'RAYS OF VICTORY' SERIES

<u>ON THE HAMMOCK:</u>

WITH THE OIL OF GRACE

FOR INDIVIDUAL VICTORY OVER RACISM

A Meditation Journal
[40 Days of Daily Meditation]
(Volume 2)

By

Dr. Jacyee Aniagolu-Johnson

First Paperback Edition
ISBN 978-0-9789669-9-7

'RAYS OF VICTORY' SERIES

ONE ON ONE WITH GOD

FOR VICTORY OVER RACISM

Daily Prayer Conversations With God for Individual Victory Over Racism

By

Dr. Jacyee Aniagolu-Johnson

First Paperback Edition:
ISBN 978-0-9789669-7-3

'RAYS OF VICTORY' SERIES

My Rays of Victory

BIBLE STUDY DIARY

A Unique Diary for your Signature Penmanship as you Triumph Over Racism

By

Dr. Jacyee Aniagolu-Johnson

First Paperback Edition:
ISBN: 978-0-9789669-4-2

Rays of Victory Series

Correspondence:

Please send Correspondence to:

Marble Tower Publishing

P.O. Box 1654, Laurel, Maryland 20725

OR

Submit a Contact Request Form at:

www.marbletowerpublishing.com

www.ravbookseries.com

www.ingramcontent.com/pod-product-compliance
Lightning Source LLC
LaVergne TN
LVHW051226080426
835513LV00016B/1443